Reading SRA Mastery Plus

Teacher's Guide

Level 3

Siegfried Engelmann
Susan Hanner

SRA

A Division of The McGraw-Hill Companies

Columbus, Ohio

Which *Reading Mastery* Program Is Right for Your Students?

Reading Mastery Plus, Level 3, is used as part of the *Reading Mastery Plus* option and as part of the *Reading Mastery Classic* option. The difference between the Plus option and the Classic option is simply the number of components that are included in the program. The Plus option is a language-arts program. The Classic option is a core reading program that does not have all the components that are in the Plus option. Below is a comparison of the components that are used for the Classic option and the Plus option. If you select the Classic option, your program will consist of everything in the first column. If you want to expand it, you may select from the boldfaced items in the second column. If you select the *Reading Mastery Plus* option, all the components are included.

The pages that follow in this guide are based on the Plus option and assume that all the components are used. If you're using the Classic option, skip those parts of the guide that refer to the optional language-arts components. These are the boldfaced items shown in the second column.

Level 3

Reading Mastery Classic Option

- Three Presentation Books
- Answer Key
- Writing and Spelling Guide
- Teacher's Guide
- Three Textbooks
- Three Workbooks

Reading Mastery Plus Option

- Three Presentation Books
- Answer Key
- Writing and Spelling Guide
- Teacher's Guide
- Three Textbooks
- Three Workbooks

- **Language Arts Guide**
- **Activities Across the Curriculum**
- **Literature Guide**
- **Literature Anthology**

Acknowledgments

The authors are grateful to the following people for their input in the field-testing and preparation of Level 3.

Laurie Anders

Sandy Bayless

Pat Pielaet

Mary Rosenbaum

Peggy Peterson

www.sra4kids.com

SRA/McGraw-Hill

A Division of The McGraw-Hill Companies

Copyright © 2002 by SRA/McGraw-Hill.

Send all inquiries to:
SRA/McGraw-Hill
4400 Easton Commons
Columbus, OH 43219

Printed in the United States of America.

ISBN 0-07-569132-9

7 8 9 10 11 12 POH 10 09 08 07

Contents

The lessons for *Reading Mastery Plus* Level 3 provide virtually all the specific information that you need to present them. The purpose of this guide is not to repeat the specific directions that appear in the lessons, but to explain the rationale for the procedures and to provide the kind of information that you will probably need to deal with specific problems.

Introduction

Reading Mastery Plus Level 3 is a one-year program containing 145 lessons that are designed to follow *Reading Mastery Plus* Level 2. All levels of *Reading Mastery Plus* are research-based sequences that have been thoroughly field-tested and revised on the basis of performance of teachers and students.

Following completion of *Reading Mastery Plus* Level 3, students may go into a variety of programs. They may continue with structured reading. One such option, which is continuous with the skills and formats of Level 3, is *Reading Mastery Plus* Level 4.

In any case, the students who complete Level 3 will have solid decoding skills, a relatively large reading vocabulary, and a good working knowledge of word meanings. The most important attribute students will have, however, is skill in **reading to learn.** They will be well-practiced in learning new concepts and gleaning new information from texts that they read, rather than from accompanying discussions. Their ability to "read to learn" enables them to engage in a variety of sophisticated projects involving research and reading on a variety of topics.

Many students who fail to become good functional readers have not received the kind of practice and perspectives necessary to develop proficiency in reading to learn. Their reading programs concentrated almost exclusively on stories, simple information passages, and literature.

In contrast, *Reading Mastery Plus* Level 3 provides a very strong focus on the skills needed for students to become proficient at letting a textbook or article "teach" them something that may involve rules and evidence.

Facts About the Program

For Whom

Reading Mastery Plus Level 3 is appropriate for students who have completed *Reading Mastery Plus* Level 2. It also may be used for any student who reads at about beginning third-grade level. The placement test that appears in Appendix A of this guide may be used to determine whether students meet the criteria for placement in *Reading Mastery Plus* Level 3.

Program Components

Teacher Support

The following teacher materials are included in *Reading Mastery Plus* Level 3:

- **3 presentation books** provide specific teacher instructions for presenting every activity in the program.

- **An Answer Key book** contains answer keys for worksheet and textbook responses.

- **The Teacher's Guide** provides a complete explanation of the program and how to teach it. Explanations of the program components indicate skills students learn. The guide provides suggestions for teaching critical exercises and for correcting more typical mistakes. The guide also discusses the in-program tests and specifies remedies for students who do not perform acceptably on these tests. The guide's Appendices include a list of spelling words, glossary, placement test, summary sheets, and

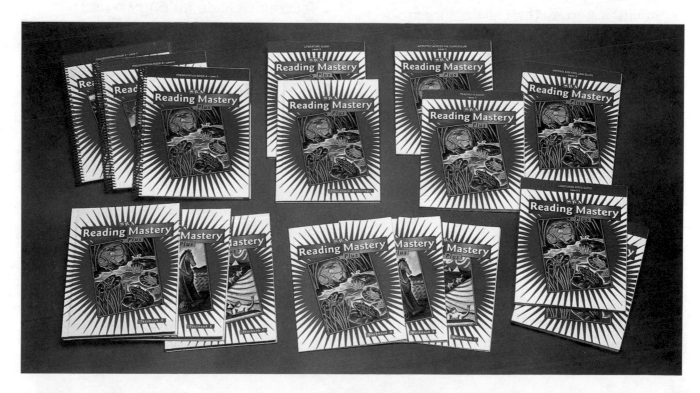

reproducible blackline masters used in teaching the program. Blackline masters of family letters are also supplied to be sent home twice during the school year.

- **The Literature Guide** provides directions and blackline masters for activities that are specified for the 16 literature selections that students read and the one "read-to" selection. For most literature lessons, students learn the new vocabulary that is in the selection, read the selection, answer questions, and do one or more expansion activities.

- **The Writing-Spelling Guide** provides scripted material for directing the activities for 131 writing-spelling lessons.

- **The Language Arts Guide** provides directions and blackline masters for the further development of selected reading-related skills. These exercises begin on lesson 51 and run every day through lesson 140.

- **Activities Across the Curriculum** provides directions and blackline masters for 39 activities that can be used throughout the program to extend and reinforce the skills that the students are acquiring.

Student Materials

The following student materials are included in *Reading Mastery Plus* Level 3:

- **3 textbooks** with 4-color illustrations contain vocabulary lists, stories, and information passages that students read as part of every reading lesson, comprehension items for the stories and the information passages presented in the lessons, and tests 1–15.

- **Worksheets for daily lessons** provide additional comprehension activities, which are coordinated with the textbook stories.

- **A literature anthology** is used in 15 of the 16 literature lessons to reinforce the skills students learn in the reading program and to enrich their experiences with literature.

- **Blackline masters** appearing in this guide, in the Literature Guide, and in the Language Arts Guide are to be reproduced for fact-game activities, literature-lesson activities, and other selected reading-related skills.

Home Connection

- **Two blackline masters** are supplied for family letters to be sent home twice a year. See Appendix K in the Teacher's Guide for English and Spanish versions.

Scheduling Lessons

The program includes daily reading lessons, daily lessons in writing-spelling, and (starting at lesson 51, and continuing through lesson 140) daily lessons for reading-related skills. The program also includes intermittent project lessons and literature lessons.

Daily reading lessons require 40 minutes each. They address core reading skills—decoding, comprehension, and skills in "reading to learn." The anticipated rate is that students complete one lesson per day.

Daily independent-work periods require 30 minutes each. Students need this in-school time to complete the independent work presented in the daily reading lessons.

Daily writing-spelling lessons require 10 minutes each. They should not be scheduled in the 40 minutes allocated for the daily reading lessons. Ideally, they should occur at another time of the school day.

Each lesson in the Language Arts Guide requires 10 to 15 minutes. The lessons provide time for students to complete independent work and for the workcheck of that work. These lessons should not be scheduled in the 40 minutes allowed for the daily reading lesson.

The time required to complete the activities in Activities Across the Curriculum varies from approximately 10 minutes to about an hour. These activities should be scheduled outside of the daily reading lesson.

Each project lesson and literature lesson requires 40 to 80 minutes; however, some projects could require even more time. These lessons should not be scheduled as part of the daily reading period, but should occur at other times.

Also, **a daily workcheck period of 10 minutes** is highly desirable. This time could be scheduled at a time other than the reading period or could be added to the beginning of the reading period (making the reading period 50 minutes per day).

An efficient scheduling option has a daily 40-minute period in the morning for presenting the regular reading lesson and a daily 20-minute period in the afternoon devoted to writing, spelling, and a workcheck of the students' independent work.

The chart below summarizes the time requirements for teaching *Reading Mastery Plus* Level 3 effectively:

Time needed	Lesson type	How often
40 minutes	Reading lesson	Daily
30 minutes	Independent-work	Daily
10 minutes	Writing-spelling	Daily
10 to 15 minutes	Language Arts lesson	Daily from lesson 51–140
10 minutes	Workcheck	Daily
40 to 80 minutes	Project lesson	After every major story sequence
10 to 60 minutes	Activity lesson	From time to time
40 to 80 minutes	Literature lesson	Every 10 lessons and lessons 6 and 115

Lesson Types

Reading Mastery Plus Level 3 has eight lesson types. Some are main lessons, and some are supplemental. The following chart summarizes the lesson types:

Main Lessons (1–145):	
Number	Type
118	Reading lessons (lessons 1–9, 11–14, 16–19, 21–24, etc.).
14	Reading lessons plus individual reading checkouts (every 10 lessons: 15, 25, 35, etc.).
15	Test lessons (every 10 lessons: 10, 20, 30, etc. plus End-of-Program test. Test lessons include individual reading check-outs.).
131	Writing-spelling lessons (1–145, part of every reading lesson except test lessons).

Supplemental Lessons (10–145):	
90	Language Arts lessons (part of every reading lesson from lesson 51 through lesson 140)
16	Literature lessons (following every tenth lesson: 10, 20, etc, plus lessons 6 and 115.).
15	Special project lessons (following every major story sequence).
39	Activity lessons (from time to time)

For reading and writing-spelling, the main lessons are to be presented daily. (Only the reading lessons are to be presented during the daily 40-minute reading periods. All other lessons—writing-spelling, literature, language arts, and special-project lessons—are to be presented during some other time of the school day.)

Reading Lessons

The teaching structures of the 145 numbered reading lessons fall into three types.

1. The first is the **regular reading lesson,** which generally consists of word attack exercises, vocabulary exercises, and one or more selections that students read during the period.

2. The second lesson type consists of a **regular reading lesson, plus a reading checkout,** during which students individually read a 100-word passage from the preceding lesson.

3. The third type of reading lesson is the **test lesson,** which occurs every tenth lesson. The test lesson assesses the students' performance on both the content presented in the preceding nine lessons, and rate and accuracy in

reading a 100-word passage. Starting with lesson 30, students also play a fact game as part of the test lesson. The facts are taken from the preceding nine lessons.

Writing-Spelling Lessons

Daily writing-spelling lessons are presented beginning with lesson 1. These require about 10 minutes per lesson and involve no printed student material.

The writing-spelling lessons are numbered because they are to be coordinated with the reading lessons. The writing-spelling lessons should be presented either on the same day as the corresponding reading lesson or on a later day. The writing-spelling lessons should **not** be presented in advance of the reading lessons.

Literature Lessons

Literature lessons present stories, poems, and a play. These lessons occur every tenth lesson, starting with lesson 10, plus lessons 6 and 115. Literature lessons generally require a time period of 40 to 80 minutes, and may require more than one day to complete. The scheduled reading periods should **not** be used for presenting literature lessons.

During most literature lessons students read a selection, respond to comprehension questions about the selection, and do related activities, which may include conducting further research or engaging in a class project.

Special-Project Lessons

The 13 special-project lessons and a scavenger hunt occur intermittently, usually after students complete a major story sequence in the reading program. The special projects and the necessary materials are listed in Appendix B. The projects include making a map of a story location, completing the lyrics for a song, and acting out part of a story. The work on each project derives from rules and information that students have already mastered in the reading lessons. Some projects may require more than 80 minutes, and may take more than one day to complete. Some projects may require using computers to answer specific questions that are difficult to research through encyclopedias. (Web sites such as Ask.com are able to handle almost any question.) Some of the later projects may be started in class and then completed as homework assignments.

The special projects expand on the unique emphases of each major story sequence. The special projects: (1) provide students with information that amplifies rules or perspectives presented in main stories; (2) provide experience with cooperative learning; (3) give students an opportunity to work independently at finding information; (4) engage students in activities that reinforce self-expression.

The cycle guarantees that students learn that information applies to different contexts, that information serves as a basis for drawing inferences, and that comprehension and enjoyment of stories increases when inferences are drawn.

Language Arts Guide Lessons

Daily lessons are presented from the Language Arts Guide beginning with lesson 51. These require about 10 minutes per lesson. Most lessons involve the use of blackline masters that need to be reproduced. These lessons should be presented at a time other than that scheduled for the daily reading lesson.

Activity Lessons

The lessons provide 39 activities, most of which have blackline master student material. Each activity is keyed to a specific lesson range in *Reading Mastery Plus* Level 3. The activities cover a range of content areas, including science, social studies, and geography.

Each activity expands on the skills or information presented in the specified lessons of *Reading Mastery Plus* Level 3. Each activity specifies the content area being explored, the materials required, and the objective.

To use the activity lessons:

- Select the activities that you wish to present and schedule them at a time when the students have completed the targeted lessons in *Reading Mastery Plus* Level 3.

- Schedule sufficient time for the activity, but don't allow so much time that activity work seriously impedes students' progress through *Reading Mastery Plus* Level 3.

- Provide students with copies of blackline masters required for most activities.

Lesson Events

The following chart shows the lesson events for each type of reading lesson. The events are listed in the order of their occurrence during the lesson. Xs indicate which events occur in lessons. Xs in parentheses indicate that the lesson event does not occur in every lesson. For example, the parentheses around the Xs for **comprehension passage** indicate that the comprehension passages do not appear in every lesson; however, when they do appear, they are presented immediately before the main-story reading.

Here is a summary of the events for **regular lessons:**

- **Oral vocabulary practice**—teacher directed. Students learn and review words and expressions that will be used in later reading selections.

- **Word-attack presentation**—teacher directed. The students read lists of words aloud and do word-meaning activities with some of the words.

- **Comprehension passage**—teacher directed. The students orally read a short passage that presents information to be used in later reading activities. The students orally respond to specified tasks about key details of the comprehension passage.

- **Main-story reading**—teacher directed. Main stories are the primary teacher-directed activity in every regular lesson. The students orally read a long selection (between 280 and 850 words) and orally respond to specific comprehension tasks the teacher presents. Nearly all main stories have more than one part. Parts are presented on consecutive regular lessons. Some main stories (such as Eric and Tom) span more than 10 lessons. The story comprehension items refer to earlier parts as well as the part presented in the current lesson.

- **Paired practice.** This activity is part of each regular lesson and part of

Lesson Events	Regular Lesson	Checkout Lesson	Test Lesson
Oral vocabulary practice	(X)	(X)	
Word-attack presentation	X	X	
Comprehension passage	(X)	(X)	
Main-story reading	X	X	
Paired practice	X		
Independent work	X	X	
Workcheck	X	X	
Individual reading checkout		X	X
Fact game			X (starting in lesson 30)
Test of program content			X

some checkout lessons. It occurs immediately after the reading of the main story. Students work in pairs and read a specified part of that story to their partner. For paired practice, students are permanently assigned as either the A member or the B member of the pair. On alternate days, the A member reads the first part of the specified passage, and the B member reads the second part.

- **Independent work.** Students write answers to written items relating to (a) the comprehension passage, (b) the main story, (c) previously taught content, and (d) skills that students have learned (vocabulary words, deductions, sequencing, etc.). For typical lessons, some independent work appears on the student worksheet and some in the student textbook.

- **Workcheck**—teacher directed. The teacher (a) checks the students' independent work and (b) makes sure the students understand and correct the items they missed.

Checkout lessons occur every tenth lesson, starting with lesson 15. Students individually read a passage from the main story that was presented in the preceding lesson. Checkout lessons are designed to give the students practice in meeting rate and accuracy criteria for oral reading.

Test lessons occur every tenth lesson, starting with lesson 10. Test lessons consist of items that test students' comprehension of the new vocabulary, information, rules, and other skills that were presented in the preceding nine lessons. Starting with lesson 20, the lessons also present a rate-and-accuracy checkout on a one-hundred-word passage from the preceding lesson.

Starting with lesson 30, students also play a **fact game** in test lessons. These games provide students with practice on important facts presented in the preceding nine lessons.

Grouping the Students

If the ability level of students in the classroom is fairly homogeneous, *Reading Mastery Plus* Level 3 may be presented to the entire class. One problem with large entire-class instruction is that the individual students do not receive as many opportunities to read aloud. For this reason, you may decide to place the most able students in one group and the lower performers in another group. All students now receive more practice with supervised reading.

The placement test that appears in Appendix A of this guide may be used to evaluate each student's entry level. Directions for administering the test and criteria for placing students in the program accompany the test.

Overview of Decoding and Comprehension Emphases

Each lesson in *Reading Mastery Plus* Level 3 has two distinct objectives: one is decoding, the other is comprehension. The word-attack presentation deals not only with teaching decoding skills, but also with developing understanding of key words. Similarly, the comprehension passage and the main story are not simply vehicles for comprehension; important decoding objectives are also met through these activities.

The following outline summarizes the activities involved in the development of decoding rate and accuracy and the development of various comprehension skills. The outline specifies the part of the lesson or the material that develops each subskill.

I. DECODING EMPHASIS

A. Word-Attack Exercises (presented during the first part of each lesson)

1. *New hard words* are modeled by the teacher and then decoded by the students.

2. *Words with similar features* (for example, all end in **S,** all have the combination **oi,** or all are compound words) are grouped together in columns and are read by the students.

3. *Unrelated decodable words* (those that have been presented earlier or those that should be decodable by virtue of the students' skills) are grouped in columns.

B. Main-Story Reading Procedures (presented with the main selection for each lesson)

1. Students orally read two or three sentences for each turn.

2. Corrections for decoding errors are provided immediately. The teacher identifies the missed word, and the student rereads the sentence in which the word appears.

3. Students read the last part of the selection silently (starting in lesson 92).

Note: Procedures 1 and 2 also apply to the comprehension passage.

C. *Paired Practice*

Permanently assigned pairs of students orally reread the main story to each other. Partners are to correct each other's decoding errors.

D. *Fifth-Lesson Individual Reading Checkouts*

Students individually read a one-hundred-word passage selected from the main story of the preceding lesson and meet a specified rate-accuracy criterion.

II. COMPREHENSION EMPHASIS

A. *Vocabulary Model Sentences*
Selected vocabulary words appear in sentences like "She <u>survived</u> until she was <u>rescued</u>."

1. Students learn what each sentence means and practice saying the sentence.

2. Students respond to tasks about the meaning of specific words.

B. *Word-Attack*

Critical vocabulary items (idioms, phrases, and individual words that will appear in stories or comprehension passages) are pretaught. The teacher tells the meaning of each vocabulary word or models how to use it.

C. *Comprehension-Passage Reading*
(These passages preteach information that will appear in main stories.)

1. As the students read each passage aloud, the teacher presents specified comprehension tasks.

2. The students respond orally.

D. *Main-Story Reading Activities*

1. As the students read the story, the teacher presents specified comprehension tasks. The students respond orally.

2. The teacher presents a variety of tasks requiring recall of information, application of rules, inferences based on specific facts, and inferences based on information about different characters.

E. *Independent-Work Applications*

The students independently write answers to items that appear on the worksheets and in the textbook.

1. Some items relate to the main story that the group read.

2. If the lesson contains a comprehension passage, some items relate to the information presented in that passage.

3. Some items relate to skills (such as sequencing story events, vocabulary meanings, applying rules, alphabetizing).

4. Review items present information from earlier main stories or comprehension passages.

F. *Daily Workcheck*

　1. Independent work is checked.

　2. Students receive same-day feedback on their independent-work performance. (They receive information on the correct answers to all items.)

G. *Tenth-Lesson Fact Games* (starting in lesson 30)

　1. The students play a game in which they orally respond to comprehension items.

　2. These comprehension items cover key concepts and facts from earlier lessons. The items are particularly important because they will recur in later lessons.

H. *Tenth-Lesson Tests*

Students write answers to items that deal with rules, vocabulary meanings, and information presented in the preceding nine lessons.

The Decoding Emphasis

The decoding emphasis involves a cycle that introduces new decoding words and word families, presents these words in different story contexts, and provides practice in meeting oral reading rate-accuracy criteria. Both the decoding vocabulary and the various decoding-practice activities are coordinated in word-attack presentations, in group story readings, and, finally, in individual reading checkouts.

Students read selections that are composed entirely of words or decodable elements taught earlier in *Reading Mastery Plus* Level 3.

The Cycle for Developing Decoding Skills

The cycle for introducing a decoding word in *Reading Mastery Plus* Level 3 begins with the word appearing in the word-attack lists of two or three lessons. Then the word appears in reading selections. This development of decoding words ensures that students receive practice in reading words in sentence contexts after these words have been presented in lists.

Word-Attack Presentation

The first decoding activity in every lesson is the word-attack presentation, during which the students read ten to thirty words aloud.

• For words that appeared earlier or that are decodable the teacher asks, What word?

• Words that would probably be difficult to read are first modeled by the teacher, then read by the students. Some words are also spelled. For example: Word 1 is **actually.** What word? *Actually.* Spell **actually.** *A-C-T-U-A-L-L-Y.*

• To show students structural or phonemic similarities of different word families, the teacher presents groups of words that have common features. On page 17 are the word-attack words from lesson 52. Note that the words in columns 2 and 4 have endings, and the words in column 3 are compound words.

A

1	2	3
1. giant	1. frisky	1. <u>grand</u>children
2. special	2. blocks	2. <u>side</u>walks
3. enormous	3. bothered	3. <u>bulk</u>head
4. announcement	4. freezing	4. <u>whirl</u>pool
5. disappeared	5. checked	
	6. sparkling	

4	5	6
1. swirled	1. bow	1. early
2. tanks	2. stern	2. fuel
3. smelly	3. frost	3. thirsty
4. weighs	4. grew	4. thirstier
5. billows	5. November	

- For each word whose meaning may not be familiar to the students, the teacher gives an explanation of the meaning. Below is the teacher presentation script for column 5 of the word-attack exercise.

Column 5

y. Find column 5. ✓
- (Teacher reference:)

> 1. **bow**   4. **grew**
> 2. **stern**   5. **November**
> 3. **frost**

z. Word 1 rhymes with **how**. What word? (Signal.) *Bow.*
a. Word 2. What word? (Signal.) *Stern.*
- The bow is the front of a ship. The stern is the back of the ship. What do we call the front of a ship? (Signal.) *Bow.*
- What do we call the back of a ship? (Signal.) *Stern.*
b. Word 3. What word? (Signal.) *Frost.*
- Frost is frozen water that forms on grass during cold nights. When the temperature goes up in the morning, the frost disappears.

c. Word 4. What word? (Signal.) *Grew.*
- Word 5. What word? (Signal.) *November.*
d. Let's read those words again.
- Word 1. What word? (Signal.) *Bow.*
- (Repeat for words 2–5.)
e. (Repeat step d until firm.)

Main-Story Decoding

Following the word-attack part of the lesson, the group reads the comprehension passage and all or part of the main story aloud. As students progress through the program, less of the main story is read aloud. At first, they read only about 50 words silently. Later, they read 100 words or more.

The teacher calls on individual students to take turns, each reading two or three sentences. Every main story has an **error limit** based on two errors per hundred words in the story. If the group exceeds the error limit, the students are to reread the main story until they read within the specified error limit.

The main stories contain recently introduced words. The stories, therefore, provide word-recognition practice with these words. The error limit for the story helps the students develop effective strategies for learning new words: (1) The students quickly learn that words appearing in the word-attack lists will appear in main stories, (2) They learn that if they are to read the stories within the error limits, they should pay attention to these words when they appear in the lists.

Paired-Reading Practice

The purpose of paired reading is to provide students with an opportunity to read a relatively long passage without interruption. Although students receive oral-reading practice during the main-story reading, they usually read only two or three sentences at a time, and their reading may be interrupted with comprehension items. The paired-reading practice takes only 5 to 8 minutes for each lesson and makes a marked difference in the fluency performance of students.

Individual Reading Checkouts

Every fifth lesson includes a reading checkout, beginning with lesson 15. Students individually read a one-hundred-word passage to a checker. The purpose of the checkout is to ensure that students are progressing acceptably in oral decoding rate and accuracy. The passage that they read for the checkout is taken from the preceding lesson. To pass the checkout, the student reads the passage in less than a minute and makes no more than two errors.

The Comprehension Emphasis

Reading Mastery Plus Level 3 has a comprehension emphasis on the facts, rules, and perspectives that are presented in what the students read. The program also has a vocabulary-building emphasis.

Model sentences are the principal vehicle for expanding students' vocabulary and for introducing words that will be in upcoming selections. In addition to the model sentences, the teacher presents vocabulary information for some words as part of the word-attack exercises.

Model Vocabulary Sentences

The first model sentence is introduced in lesson 4. Others follow about every three lessons. A list of sentences appears in the back of the student textbooks (and Appendix C of this guide). Students refer to this list when learning new sentences.

Each model sentence goes through an eight-step cycle.

1. The sentence is introduced. Students read the sentence. The teacher explains the key words (two or three new words that are in the sentence). Then students answer questions about the key words. For example, for the sentence **They waded into the stream to remove tadpoles** the teacher asks these questions:

   What word tells that they got rid of something?

   What word tells that they walked through water that was not very deep?

   What's the name of baby frogs or toads?

2. Later in the same lesson in which the model sentence is introduced, students review what they have learned about the model sentence.

3. In the following lesson, students review the model sentence.

4. In the third lesson of the cycle, students review the last three model sentences that had been introduced.

5. Later in that lesson, students do written tasks in which they write answers to questions about the key words.

6. In the next lesson, students work with the two most recent sentences, which are presented with key words missing. Students write the complete sentences. (For example, the model sentence would appear as: They ▆▆ into the stream to ▆▆ ▆▆.)

7. A verbal exercise appears periodically. The teacher says part of the sentence but stops just before a key word. Students say the next word.

8. The test in every tenth lesson contains skill items that assess the students' knowledge of vocabulary words presented in the model sentences that were introduced and sufficiently reviewed during the preceding nine lessons.

Vocabulary During Word Attack

The teacher script provides "definitions" for those words that students may not know. These descriptions often show the students how to use the word. There is no attempt to provide students with **a variety of meanings of the word,** but merely to illustrate the meaning that will be used in the upcoming selection.

Here are some examples:

Impression. When you have an **impression** about something, you have an idea about that thing. If you have the **impression** that somebody is watching you, you have the idea that somebody is watching you. What's another way of saying, **She had the idea that she was working slowly?** *She had the impression that she was working slowly.*

Motion. Here's how you **motion** to come over here. (Motion.) Show me how you **motion** for somebody to move back.

Respond. When you **respond** to someone, you **answer** them. Here's another way of saying **He answered the question: He responded to the question.** What's another way of saying **He answered the question?** *He responded to the question.*

When some of these vocabulary words appear in subsequent word-attack presentations, the teacher presents tasks that require students to use the word correctly.

Definitions for all vocabulary words appear in Appendix D of this guide and at the end of textbook C.

Developing Comprehension of Facts, Rules, and Perspectives

As decoding skills are being developed through the various lesson activities, comprehension skills are also being developed for interpreting and using facts, rules, and information about unique story-character perspectives. The general skills students learn include cause and effect, literal meaning, inferential meaning, main idea, and sequencing of events. The program presents content and practice for these skills.

Here is a summary of the sequence for developing these skills:

1. Information is introduced in a comprehension passage.

2. Within two lessons of the introduction, the information is used in the main story.

3. A variation of the information also appears in the independent-work items.

4. The items are reviewed in subsequent lessons.

5. Information that is particularly important or difficult appears in the fact games or in fact reviews. The game format provides the students with massed practice on a lot of information.

6. The tenth-lesson tests assess students' understanding of the information.

7. The final step is the integration of recent information with information taught earlier. This integration provides for increasingly complex applications and review. For major story sequences, the integration culminates with a special project, in which students research additional facets of the story theme.

General Comprehension Skills

The comprehension skills that are traditionally presented in developmental reading series stress general skills such as literal comprehension, main idea, fact versus opinion, context clues, and sequencing of events. *Reading Mastery Plus* Level 3 is organized so that these skills are taught in a cumulative manner, which means that a particular skill is practiced not merely as a part of a few lessons, but is practiced repeatedly as part of many lessons. This cumulative practice ensures that the students work with the various skills in a variety of story and information contexts.

The table on page 21 summarizes the comprehension skills emphasized in each of the larger story series in *Reading Mastery Plus* Level 3. (Each story series listed spans at least three lessons.) The lesson numbers for each series are indicated in the table. If the series strongly emphasizes a particular skill, the skill is marked with an asterisk (*). If the emphasis is not as strong, it is marked with a checkmark (✓).

As the table shows, literal comprehension, cause and effect, supporting evidence, and information recall activities are part of each story series. In addition to providing practice in these four categories of comprehension skills, each story series has at least one unique focus. For example, the series about Herman the Fly (a fly who gets on a jet plane and travels around the world) presents strong comprehension emphasis on sequencing, context clues, viewpoint, supporting evidence, interpretation of feelings, map skills, reality versus fantasy, and information recall.

Table of Cumulative Comprehension Emphasis

★ = strong emphasis
✔ = not as strong

	4–6 (Little Apple Tree)	15–23 (Goad)	25–35 (Nancy)	37–52 (Herman)	54–63 (Linda & Kathy)	65–67 (Trojan Horse)	68–78 (Bertha)	86–88 (Horses)	89–106 (Andrew Dexter)	108–111 (Word Bank)	113–122 (Toby)	123–127 (Word Bank)	129–145 (Eric & Tom)
Literal comprehension	✔	✔	✔	✔	✔	✔	✔	✔	✔	✔	✔	✔	✔
Main idea	✔	★	★	✔	★	✔	✔		★	✔	✔	✔	✔
Sequencing	★	✔	✔	★	✔	✔		★	✔		★	✔	★
Cause and effect	★	★	✔	✔	✔	★	✔	✔	✔	★	✔	★	✔
Fact vs. opinion		✔			★	✔			✔	✔	★	✔	✔
Context clues		✔	★	★	✔		★		★	★	★	★	✔
Viewpoint	★	✔	★	★	✔	★	✔		★	★	★	★	★
Supporting evidence (relevant details)	★	✔	★	★	✔	✔	★	★	★	★	★	★	✔
Character development (Interpreting feelings, inferring motives, predicting behavior)	★	✔	★	★	★	✔			★	✔	★	✔	★
Map skills		★		★		✔	✔				★		★
Reality vs. fantasy	✔	★	★	★		★			★	★	✔	★	★
Information recall	✔	★	★	★	★	★	★	★	★	★	★	★	★
Reference-book skills		✔									✔		

Facts, Rules, and Perspectives

The grouping of comprehension skills according to broad traditional categories (such as supporting evidence) does not suggest the specific facts, rules, and perspectives that are introduced. Following is a summary of the facts, rules, and perspectives that are developed in *Reading Mastery Plus* Level 3. The perspectives are developed through learning the rules and facts.

The major **rules** developed in *Reading Mastery Plus* Level 3 are:

- **Measurement rules** (based on facts about centimeters, meters, miles, grams, miles per hour, seconds, degrees, inches, yards, minutes).

- **Location rules** (based on facts about the United States, Canada, Mexico, Japan, Egypt, Greece, Italy, Turkey, China, the Pacific Ocean, New York City, San Francisco, Salt Lake City, Denver, Chicago, California, Alaska, Australia).

- **History rules** (based on facts about the Trojan war, cave people, the San Francisco earthquake of 1906, future time, the Revolutionary War, Columbus discovering America, the Viking age, and ancient Greece and Egypt).

- **Classification rules** (based on facts about insects, spiders, toads and frogs, trees, types of vehicles, warm-blooded and cold-blooded animals, camels, horses, dinosaurs, kangaroos, peacocks, pigs).

- **Science rules** (based on facts about water characteristics, winds, temperature, and weather changes).

The major **perspectives** presented in *Reading Mastery Plus* Level 3 are:

- **Physical geography perspective** (earthquakes, land masses, oceans).

- **Behavior and feeling perspectives** (comparison of human and non-human responses to the same situation, projections of how the reader would behave in various situations, predictions about how a character will behave in a new situation based on information about the character's tendencies).

- **Temporal perspective** (comparison of how things were done during different historical time periods—what people thought was handsome dress in 1900, how Vikings ate, comparison of how modern people and the ancient Egyptians would move grain and other goods).

- **Size perspective** (comparison of objects viewed by average-sized beings and by very small beings—how a drop of water looks to them, how it feels to fall from a high place, how much they have to eat with respect to their body weight).

- **Distance perspective** (comparison of different trips—for instance, the distance from New York to San Francisco compared with the distance from San Francisco to Japan).

- **Place perspective** (comparison of building materials, customs, language, means of conveyance, dress of people from different places).

Preparing to Teach

This section of the guide provides you with specific, technical information about what you will be teaching and some of the problems students may have with the presentations. The purpose is to provide you with the information and the general cautions you need to **guarantee** that the students move through the program smoothly.

The guide is a tool that you should refer to throughout the year as part of your preparation for teaching the program.

1. Don't begin the program until you have studied this section of the guide.

2. Practice presenting the various exercises before you present the first lessons to the students. Don't simply read them over and assume that you will be able to present them well. Read the script aloud. Present the signals the students are to respond to. Practice saying the corrections. Make sure you can smoothly present any new exercise type that is scheduled for upcoming lessons. During the first part of the program, a fair amount of practice may be required. For later lessons, less preparation is needed.

General Teaching Strategies

When teaching *Reading Mastery Plus* Level 3 you will be engaged in various types of activities.

- You will present model sentences and word-attack exercises.

- You will direct the students in the group reading of comprehension passages and main stories. (As they read, you will present specified oral comprehension tasks.)

- You will monitor students as they do their independent work.

- You will provide a daily workcheck and record the number of errors students make on their independent work.

- For lessons that involve individual checkouts and fact games, you will monitor the checkouts and games.

- You will provide remedies for students who do not pass tenth-lesson tests.

Here is a summary of the general techniques that you will use.

Get into the lesson quickly. No discussions are necessary.

Teach to mastery. Use the following guidelines:

- Repeat tasks if students are not firm.

• Use clear signals. All signals have the same purpose: They trigger a simultaneous response from the group. All signals have the same rationale: If you get the group to respond simultaneously (with no student leading the others) you will receive good information about the performance of the students. At the same time, students will receive more frequent practice than they would using individual responses.

• Reinforce good performance. Make your praise specific. If the students have just completed a difficult word list with no errors tell them what they did: You read without any mistakes. Good for you. Praise students for following the rules you present.

Pace the exercises. Since a great deal of information must be taught during the daily presentation, it is important for you to move quickly, but not to rush the students so much that they make mistakes. To ensure a smoothly paced lesson, you should become familiar with the exercises before presenting them. You must be able to present them without having to refer to the page for every word. Fast pacing is important for the following reasons:

• It reduces the problems of managing students and maintaining on-task behavior. Studies have shown that faster pacing secures more student interest and reduces management problems.

• Fast pacing results in greater student achievement. With faster pacing, a teacher can cover more material in a fixed amount of time and provide more student practice in that time.

• Many tasks become more difficult when they are presented slowly. Slower pacing places greater memory demands on students. Faster pacing, on the other hand, reduces memory load.

Monitor independent work. Intermittently monitor students as they do their independent work. Make sure that students are working at a reasonable rate, but are not looking up answers to items and are not copying.

Using the Teacher-Presentation Scripts

The script for each lesson indicates how to present the structured activities. The lesson is a script that shows what you say, what you do, and what the students' responses are to be.

What you say appears in blue type:

You say this.

What you do appears in parentheses:

(You do this.)

The responses of the students are in italics:

Students say this.

[Individual student says this.]

Follow the specified wording in the script. While wording variations from the script are not always dangerous, you will be assured of communicating clearly with the students if you follow the script exactly. The wording in the teacher presentation books is succinctly controlled. The tasks are arranged so they focus on important aspects of what the students are to do. Although you may initially feel uncomfortable "reading" from a script, follow the scripts very closely; try to present them as if you're saying something important to the students. If you do, you'll soon find that working from a script is not difficult and that students indeed respond well to what you say.

Conventions

Samples of the teacher presentation script appear on page 27.

The arrows show the six different things you'll do that are not spelled out in the script. You'll signal to make sure that group responses involve all the students. You'll "firm" critical parts of the exercises. For some exercises, you'll write things on the board.

Arrow ❶: Signals for Group Responses
(Signal.) and (Tap.)

Some tasks call for group responses. If students respond together with brisk, unison responses, you receive good information about whether the students are performing correctly. The simplest way to

direct students to respond together is to signal or tap in a predictable cadence—just like the cadence in a musical piece. By listening carefully to the responses, you can tell both which students make mistakes and which ones respond late, copying those who responded first. As a result, you are able to correct specific mistakes, maximize the amount of practice, and evaluate the performance of each student.

Arrows labeled 1 on page 27 specify (Signal.) for the student responses **be, become,** and taps for the student spelling of **become** (a series of responses).

Using Signals

To signal the group to respond:

1. Say the task specified in the presentation script.

2. Pause.

3. Clap, or make another auditory signal such as a tap or a finger snap. (An auditory signal is necessary because the students are not looking at you but at the material they are reading.)

Here are procedures for effective signaling:

- Don't signal while talking. Talk first, then signal.

- Always maintain a time interval of about one second between the last word of the instructions or question and the signal. Signal timing should be consistent so students can respond together.

- Require students to respond together, on signal.

Column 3

k. Find column 3. ✓ ← **3**

5 → • (Teacher reference:)

1. <u>be</u>come	4. <u>sound</u>ly
2. <u>sob</u>bing	5. <u>dar</u>ling
3. <u>your</u>self	6. <u>in</u>stead

• These words have more than one syllable. The first syllable is underlined.

l. Word 1. What's the first syllable? (Signal.) *be.*

• What's the whole word? (Signal.) ← **1**
Become.

m. Word 2. What's the first syllable? (Signal.) *sob.*

• What's the whole word? (Signal.)
Sobbing.

n. Word 3. What's the first syllable? (Signal.) *your.*

• What's the whole word? (Signal.)
Yourself.

o. Word 4. What's the first syllable? (Signal.) *sound.*

• What's the whole word? (Signal.)
Soundly.

p. Word 5. What's the first syllable? (Signal.) *dar.*

• What's the whole word? (Signal.)
Darling.

q. Word 6. What's the first syllable? (Signal.) *in.*

• What's the whole word? (Signal.)
Instead.

r. Let's read those words again, the fast way.

• Word 1. What word? (Signal.) *Become.*
• (Repeat for words 2–6.) ← **5**

s. (Repeat step r until firm.) ← **2**

Column 4

t. Find column 4. ✓
• (Teacher reference:)

1. couple	4. important
2. whirl	5. expression
3. moments	6. swirl

u. Word 1. What word? (Signal.) *Couple.*
• (Repeat for words 2–6.)

v. (Repeat step u until firm.) ← **2**

Individual Turns ← **6**
(For columns 1–4: Call on individual students, each to read one to three words per turn.)

EXERCISE 1
VOCABULARY REVIEW

a. You learned a sentence about how you measure your weight.

• Everybody, say that sentence. Get ready. (Signal.) *You measure your weight in pounds.*
• (Repeat until firm.) ← **2**

EXERCISE 2
FACT REVIEW

a. Let's review some facts you have learned. First we'll go over the facts together. Then I'll call on each of you to do some facts.

b. Tell me which comes first in a storm, lightning or thunder. Get ready. (Signal.) *Lightning.*
• Tell me what is longer, a yard or a meter. Get ready. (Signal.) *A meter.*
• Tell me how long a football field is. Get ready. (Signal.) *100 yards.*
• Tell me how many centimeters are in a meter. Get ready. (Signal.) *100.*
• (Repeat step g until firm.) ← **2**

SENTENCE COPYING

a. (Write on the board:)

4 → **Toads love to eat flies.**

b. You're going to write this sentence.
• (Call on a student to read the sentence.)
c. Everybody, turn your paper over. ✓ ←
• Write the sentence on the top line.
(Observe students and give feedback.) ← **3**
d. Later you can write the sentence two more times on the lines below.

- To correct mistakes of not following the signal, show students exactly what you want them to do:

  I'm good at answering the right way.

  My turn: Spell **become.** Get ready.

  (Tap) **B**...(tap) **E**...(tap) **C**...(tap) **O**...(tap) **M**...(tap) **E.**

  Let's see who can do it just that way:

  Your turn. Spell **become.** Get ready. (Tap for each letter.) *B-E-C-O-M-E.*

- **Do not respond with the students** unless you are trying to work with them on a difficult response. You present only what is in blue. You do not say the answers with the students, and you should not move your lips or give other nonverbal clues about what the answer is.

Signals are very important early in the program. After students have learned the routine, the signals are not as critical because the students will be able to respond on cue with no signal. That will happen, however, only if you consistently present signals with the same predictable timing.

Arrow ❷ : Firming

(Repeat until firm.)

Wherever there's a signal, there's a place where students may make mistakes. You correct mistakes as soon as you hear them. A correction may occur during any part of the teacher presentation that calls for students to respond. It may also occur in connection with what students are writing.

- Mistakes on oral responses include saying the wrong thing or not responding. To correct: **You say the correct answer; then repeat the task the students missed.** For example:

  You learned a sentence about how you measure your weight. Everybody, say that sentence. Get ready. (Signal.)

If some students do not respond, respond slowly, or say an incorrect sentence, a mistake has occurred. As soon as you hear a mistake, you **say the correct answer:**

  Here's the sentence about how you measure your weight: You measure your weight in pounds.

Repeat the task:

  Everybody, say that sentence. Get ready. (Signal.)

A special correction is needed when correcting mistakes on tasks that teach a series of things. This type of correction is marked with the notation:

(Repeat step _ until firm.)

An example of this kind of task appears below. The bracket shows a section of the presentation that is to be repeated following a mistake:

EXERCISE 2

FACT REVIEW

a. Let's review some facts you have learned. First we'll go over the facts together. Then I'll call on each of you to do some facts.

b. Tell me which comes first in a storm, lightning or thunder. Get ready. (Signal.) *Lightning.*
 • Tell me what is longer, a yard or a meter. Get ready. (Signal.) *A meter.*
 • Tell me how long a football field is. Get ready. (Signal.) *100 yards.*
 • Tell me how many centimeters are in a meter. Get ready. (Signal.) *100.*
 • (Repeat step g until firm.) ←**2**

When you "repeat until firm," you follow these steps:

1. **Correct the mistake.** (Tell the answer and repeat the task that was missed.)

2. **Return to the beginning of the bracketed part and present the entire part.** For example, students miss the third task (Tell me how long a football field is.).

 You tell the answer: 100 yards.

 You repeat the task: Tell me how long a football field is.

 You return to the first task in the bracketed part and repeat the entire part: Let's go back. Tell me which comes first in a storm, lightning or thunder . . . etc.

Arrow **3** : Monitoring Students
(Observe students and give feedback.) and ✔

SENTENCE COPYING

a. (Write on the board:)

 Toads love to eat flies.

b. You're going to write this sentence.
 • (Call on a student to read the sentence.)
c. Everybody, turn your paper over. ✔ ←**3**
 • Write the sentence on the top line. (Observe students and give feedback.) ←**3**
d. Later you can write the sentence two more times on the lines below. **3**

The arrows labeled 3 show a checkmark (✔) or the direction **(Observe students and give feedback.).** These script conventions indicate how you are to monitor student performance.

The ✔ is a note to see whether the students have touched the part of the page you refer to. If you tell them to **turn their paper over,** or **touch column 2,** you check to see that they are doing that. Your check requires only a second or two. Monitor the responses of several "average performing" students. If their responses are acceptable, proceed with the presentation.

The **(Observe students and give feedback.)** direction implies a more elaborate response on your part. You sample more students and you give feedback, not only to individual students, but also to the group. Here are the basic rules for what to do and what not to do when you observe and give feedback:

 • Circulate to make sure that you can see all of the students' papers.

- **As soon as students start to work, start observing.** As you observe, make comments to the whole class. Focus these comments on students who are following directions, working quickly, and working accurately. Wow, a couple of students are almost finished. I haven't seen one mistake so far.

- When students raise their hands to indicate that they are finished, acknowledge them.

- **If you observe mistakes, do not provide a great deal of individual help.** For example, if the directions tell students to circle the answer and some students underline it, tell them, You didn't follow the directions for number 4. Read the directions and do what they say.

If there are serious problems with part of the independent work, repeat it during the next reading period. Do not proceed in the program if the students are making a high rate of errors.

Arrow ④: Board Work

What you write on the board is indicated in blue display boxes (see page 27). In the sample exercise, you write the sentence **Toads love to eat flies.**

Arrow ⑤: Script Conventions

(Repeat for words 2–6.) and **(Teacher reference:)**

Sometimes teachers lose their place in the teacher presentation script. Teachers also have difficulty keeping track of where the students are supposed to be touching in their textbooks or workbooks. Arrow 5 on page 27 shows two script conventions that enable you to more easily track what you and the students are supposed to be doing.

Step r instructs teachers "Repeat for words 2–6." Teachers are to repeat: Word ___. What word? (Signal.) Repeat for the remaining words **sobbing, yourself, soundly, darling, instead.** You don't have to read the script for those words. So you are able to attend more to what the students are doing. Here is what you would say:

r. Let's read those words again, the fast way.
- Word 1. What word? (Signal.) *Become.*
- Word 2. What word? (Signal.) *Sobbing.*
- Word 3. What word? (Signal.) *Yourself.*
- Word 4. What word? (Signal.) *Soundly.*
- Word 5. What word? (Signal.) *Darling.*
- Word 6. What word? (Signal.) *Instead.*

The presentation script provides a teacher reference that shows the students' material.

→ • (Teacher reference:)

1. become	4. soundly
2. sobbing	5. darling
3. yourself	6. instead

Refer to the teacher references as you monitor students' responses to this activity.

By looking at the teacher reference you don't have to peek at a student's textbook to see what the next word is. Using teacher references can help free you from the script without straying from the wording the script specifies. For most word lists, you'll use the same wording for all words. Once you know the wording (specified for the first word in the list) you can use the teacher reference to follow the same format shown for the first word to direct the other words.

Arrow ⑥ : Individual Turns

Individual turns occur routinely as part of a word-attack presentation that has more than one column of words. Several other structured exercise types, such as fact reviews, also call for individual turns.

Think of individual turns as a diagnostic tool that lets you know if the students are firm on the material you just presented to the group. The general procedure for presenting individual turns is to present them only when you think the students are firm on the group tasks.

Call on a sufficient number of individual students to let you know whether they have mastered the content. You should not try to give every student a turn on every task, but rather you should sample the group in a way that does not consume a lot of time. If there are 25 students in the group, you might present tasks to 7 students. Of these 7, sample 4 students who may be weak on the material and 3 others. If students in this sample are firm, the others in the group are probably also firm.

Teaching to the Group

If the group has problems, you'll correct their mistakes or firm students on the content that has not been mastered. If the group is firm, you'll speed up the presentation and move on.

To adjust the presentation to the performance of the group, you have to attend to individuals within the group. Although all the students are supposed to have the skills needed to perform well in *Reading Mastery Plus* Level 3, there will be a range of individual variation.

This range in ability raises a question about whether you should adjust your presentation to the higher performers in the group, those in the middle, or the lower performers. Here are the guidelines:

- **If some students should not really be in the group** (according to their placement-test performance or performance on the lessons), **do not teach to them.** Either place them in a group that is appropriate for their performance level, or try to find a way to give them additional practice outside of the scheduled reading period. (One plan that may work is to have them read to a higher-performing student on a daily basis.)

- **If all students are appropriately placed, teach to the students who tend to be lower but who tend not to be the slowest in the group.** If you teach to the slowest, you may make the presentation tedious for most of the other students, and you will not move through the lessons as quickly as you should. If you teach to the higher performers, you will make it difficult for possibly half of the students. However, if you gauge your presentation to the performance of the lower students, you will provide a little more practice than the higher students require, but the presentation will not be significantly slowed for them. The presentation will also be careful enough that the lowest students in the group will benefit from it about 80 percent of the time. At that level, they will master the material (even if they need some additional practice).

• **Provide students with very unambiguous models of what you expect them to do.** Do not praise them for sloppy approximations, but also do not lose patience with them. Repeat material until they can perform perfectly. Unless you provide such a model, you're asking students to improve when they are not exactly sure what constitutes improvement.

• **Expect students to accelerate.** If you place students appropriately, initially teach them to a very hard criterion of performance, and show them what you expect them to do, they will learn faster and faster. Furthermore, they will enjoy learning much more.

Teaching the Lessons

This section gives information about teaching each part of the lesson.

Vocabulary Exercises

General Information

These exercises are the first in the lesson. They focus on model sentences and the meaning of several key words. The activities are oral. The expectation is that the students will perform very well on the exercises. Students should not require much time to respond, and their responses should be correct.

The exercise below is from lesson 37. The exercise introduces the vocabulary sentence: **Several paths continued for a great distance.** The key words are **several, continued, distance.** The focus is on the specific meaning used in the vocabulary sentence.

EXERCISE 1

VOCABULARY

a. **Find page 338 in your textbook.** ✓
  • Touch sentence 9. ✓
  • This is a new vocabulary sentence. It says: Several paths continued for a great distance. Everybody, read that sentence. Get ready. (Signal.) *Several paths continued for a great distance.*
  ⌐ • Close your eyes and say the sentence. Get ready. (Signal.) *Several paths continued for a great distance.*
  ⌐ • (Repeat until firm.)

b. The sentence says that **several** paths continued. That's more than two paths but less than many paths. Maybe there were four paths, maybe there were three or five. There were not fifty paths.

c. Several paths **continued.** If they continued, they kept on going. What's another word for **kept on going?** (Signal.) *Continued.*

d. A great distance is a very long way. The paths went for many miles. If the paths went for a **short** distance, they would not go very far. What's another way of saying **a very long way?** (Signal.) *A great distance.*

e. Listen: Several paths continued for a great distance.
  ⌐ • Everybody, say the sentence. Get ready. (Signal.) *Several paths continued for a great distance.*
  ⌐ • (Repeat until firm.)

  ⌐ f. What word refers to more than two but less than a lot? (Signal.) *Several.*
  • What word means **kept on going?** (Signal.) *Continued.*
  • What part means **a long way?** (Signal.) *A great distance.*
  ⌐ • (Repeat step f until firm.)

Presenting Vocabulary Exercises

Follow these guidelines when presenting the exercises.

1. Make sure that the students produce good unison responses. Don't permit droning responses when students say the sentence.

2. Make sure that students are firm in saying the sentence. In step a, you repeat the sentence until firm. For

some sentences, students may have to say it three or more times. If students are not firm in saying the sentence, however, they will have problems when the sentence is used in this lesson and reviewed in later lessons.

3. Don't make repeating the sentence seem like punishment. If you respond to these exercises as fun or challenges that you look forward to, the students will respond the same way. Keep it upbeat and fast moving: Once more. Get ready . . .

4. Make sure students are firm on what the key words mean. In step f, you present questions about the key words. If students are not perfectly firm on all the answers, they'll have problems later. So don't be afraid to repeat items that have weak responses. And don't be afraid to use individual turns for students that produce weak or questionable responses.

5. Use the vocabulary review tasks as an indicator of how well students learn the new material. The review task below is presented later in lesson 37 and serves as a delayed test on the new sentence. If students do not do well on these same-day reviews, you may need to provide more practice on the exercises that introduce the sentences. (This review task is also presented in the next lesson.)

EXERCISE 3

VOCABULARY REVIEW

a. Here's the new vocabulary sentence: Several paths continued for a great distance.

- • Everybody, say the sentence. Get ready. (Signal.) *Several paths continued for a great distance.*
- • (Repeat until firm.)
 b. What word means **kept on going?** (Signal.) *Continued.*
- • What word refers to more than two but less than a lot? (Signal.) *Several.*
- • What part means **a long way?** (Signal.) *A great distance.*

6. Expect student performance to improve **if you bring them to mastery in the early lessons.** You'll find that they tend to learn new sentences with less repetition. You can often provide far less practice and maintain a far less strict criterion of performance. Occasionally, students will need firming, but they will tend to learn the sentences much faster than they do at first.

Word-Attack Exercises

General Information

The words the students are to read during the word-attack portion of the lesson appear in the textbook. The words are in columns, each containing four to six words.

The main purpose of the word-attack exercises is to teach students the new words that will appear in the stories and information passages they read. For words that students probably understand, there is no work on word meaning. For words that may be unfamiliar to the students, you'll tell the meaning of the word or show how to use the word in a sentence. The words that have a meaning emphasis are scattered throughout the lists. In the sample below from lesson 46, there are four words for which you provide information about meaning. (Three are in column 1, one is in column 4.)

1	2	3
1. strength	1. sprayed	1. several
2. human	2. cleared	2. continue
3. mountain	3. cooled	3. corners
4. excitement	4. napped	4. hairy
5. California		5. enemy

4	5
1. Pacific Ocean	1. cross
2. globe	2. Japan
3. jet's	3. attention
4. free	4. closets
5. web	5. mean-looking
6. strip	6. moments

EXERCISE 2

READING WORDS

Column 1

a. **Find lesson 46 in your textbook.** ✓
- Touch column 1. ✓
- (Teacher reference:)

1. strength	4. excitement
2. human	5. California
3. mountain	

b. Word 1 is **strength.** What word? (Signal.) *Strength.*
- Spell **strength.** Get ready. (Tap for each letter.) *S-T-R-E-N-G-T-H.*
- Your strength is how strong you are. A person who is stronger has more strength. Who has more strength, a child or a grown-up? (Signal.) *A grown-up.*

c. Word 2 is **human.** What word? (Signal.) *Human.*
- Spell **human.** Get ready. (Tap for each letter.) *H-U-M-A-N.*
- Humans are people. Here's another way of saying **There were many people in the woods: There were many humans in the woods.**

d. Word 3 is **mountain.** What word? (Signal.) *Mountain.*
- Spell **mountain.** Get ready. (Tap for each letter.) *M-O-U-N-T-A-I-N.*

e. Word 4 is **excitement.** What word? (Signal.) *Excitement.*
- When you are worked up and have trouble sitting still, you feel excitement.

f. Word 5 is **California.** What word? (Signal.) *California.*

g. Let's read those words again, the fast way.
- Word 1. What word? (Signal.) *Strength.*
- (Repeat for words 2–5.)

h. (Repeat step g until firm.)

Column 2

i. Find column 2. ✓
- (Teacher reference:)

1. sprayed	3. cooled
2. cleared	4. napped

- All these words end with the letters **E-D.**

j. Word 1. What word? (Signal.) *Sprayed.*
- (Repeat for words 2–4.)

k. Let's read those words again.
- Word 1. What word? (Signal.) *Sprayed.*
- (Repeat for words 2–4.)

l. (Repeat step k until firm.)

Column 3

m. Find column 3. ✓
- (Teacher reference:)

> | | |
> |---|---|
> | 1. **se**veral | 4. **hair**y |
> | 2. **con**tinue | 5. **en**emy |
> | 3. **corn**ers | |

- These words have more than one syllable. The first syllable is underlined.

n. Word 1. What's the first syllable? (Signal.) *sev.*
- What's the whole word? (Signal.) *Several.*
- If several people are meeting, could there be three people? (Signal.) *Yes.*
- Could there be four people? (Signal.) *Yes.*
- Could there be two people? (Signal.) *No.*
- Could there be a lot of people? (Signal.) *No.*

o. Word 2. What's the first syllable? (Signal.) *con.*
- What's the whole word? (Signal.) *Continue.*
- What do you do when you keep on working? (Signal.) *Continue working.*

p. Word 3. What's the first syllable? (Signal.) *corn.*
- What's the whole word? (Signal.) *Corners.*

q. Word 4. What's the first syllable? (Signal.) *hair.*
- What's the whole word? (Signal.) *Hairy.*

r. Word 5. What's the first syllable? (Signal.) *en.*
- What's the whole word? (Signal.) *Enemy.*

s. Let's read those words again.
- Word 1. What word? (Signal.) *Several.*
- (Repeat for: **2. continue, 3. corners, 4. hairy, 5. enemy.**)

t. (Repeat step s until firm.)

Column 4

u. Find column 4. ✓
- (Teacher reference:)

> | | |
> |---|---|
> | 1. **Pacific Ocean** | 4. **free** |
> | 2. **globe** | 5. **web** |
> | 3. **jet's** | 6. **strip** |

v. Number 1. What words? (Signal.) *Pacific Ocean.*
- Is the Pacific Ocean on the **east** coast or the **west** coast of the United States? (Signal.) *West.*

w. Word 2. What word? (Signal.) *Globe.*
- A small model of Earth is called a globe. A globe is shaped like a ball.

x. Word 3. What word? (Signal.) *Jet's.*
- (Repeat for words 4–6.)

y. Let's read those words again.
- Number 1. What words? (Signal.) *Pacific Ocean.*
- Word 2. What word? (Signal.) *Globe.*
- (Repeat for words 3–6.)

z. (Repeat step y until firm.)

Column 5

a. Find column 5. ✓
- (Teacher reference:)

> | | |
> |---|---|
> | 1. **cross** | 4. **closets** |
> | 2. **Japan** | 5. **mean-looking** |
> | 3. **attention** | 6. **moments** |

b. Word 1. What word? (Signal.) *Cross.*
- (Repeat for words 2–6.)

c. Let's read those words again.
- Word 1. What word? (Signal.) *Cross.*
- (Repeat for words 2–6.)

d. (Repeat step c until firm.)

Individual Turns

(For columns 1–5: Call on individual students, each to read one to three words per turn.)

The individual lists have different decoding emphases. In the previous sample, column 1 presents words that are difficult to decode. These words are modeled before students read them. The students also spell some of these words. (Note that students never spell more than four words per lesson.)

Columns 2 through 5 present decodable words that require no modeling. The words in column 2 have endings. Column 3 presents multisyllabic words. The first component in each word is underlined. The presentation for these words requires students to attend to the components. (First they read the underlined part of the word; then they read the whole word.) The words in columns 4 and 5 are miscellaneous, decodable words that will appear in the reading selections. For all these words you, (1) indicate the number of the word students are to read; (2) say What word?; (3) then signal. For example, for word 1 you say, Word 1. What word? When you say word 1, students are to touch under the word. When you say, What word? they are to say the word.

The arrangement and focus of the various columns change from one lesson to another. In some lessons, words that have a particular sound feature will be grouped in a column—for instance, words that have the letter combinations **ce** or **ge**. Students spell some words, but never more than four per lesson. Some lists focus on various types of multisyllabic words. Some lists focus on endings. And some lists have no particular focus except that the words will appear in an upcoming reading selection.

The amount of drill and practice that you provide should depend on how well students read selections. If their reading is accurate and fluent (students reading at close to a conversational rate and not generally exceeding the error limit), you can usually go through the word lists very quickly and with very little repetition. If there are some students in the group who are a little weak, give them more individual turns. But do not try to give all students individual turns.

Presenting Word-Attack Exercises

Maintain clear signals. Use a clap or some other *auditory* signal to indicate when the students are to respond. Your signal should follow the last word of the task by one second. The timing should always be the same—very rhythmical and predictable.

Correct signal violations early in the program. If the students do not respond on signal, tell them what they did or what they should do: Wait for the signal, or You're late. Then repeat the task, reinforcing the students if they respond on signal. Once you know that the students are firm, you can relax the corrections on signal violations, but don't let the students get so sloppy that you can't clearly hear their responses.

Correct droning, sing-song responses. Tell students, Say it the way you talk. Model the correct behavior and enforce it. Also, check your pacing and make sure you model responses in a normal speaking voice.

Confirm all words that are read correctly by the group. This is important early in the program. For example, immediately after the group reads the word **information,** say, Yes, information. This practice guards against the possibility that some students misread the word but that you didn't hear the misreading.

Correct all word-reading errors immediately. Even if only one student in the group makes an error, say the correct word.

Work within a specified time frame. The word-attack portion of the lesson takes more time on some days than on others. However, even in the longest lessons, *the word-attack portion should not take more than seven or eight minutes.*

Position yourself so you can observe what students are doing. If you are working with a large group of students, do not stand in front of the group as you present the word-attack exercises. Instead, walk among the students. When you stand behind them and look over their shoulders, you can see whether they are pointing to the appropriate words, and you can observe their responses better than if you are in front of them.

A good procedure is to focus on six to eight individual students. Stand behind one of them as you present two or three words. Then move behind another one. Select the students that probably would make mistakes. Observe whether they are:

- pointing to the appropriate words
- saying the correct words
- initiating the response on signal or waiting for others to lead them

Regular Reading Selections

Reading Mastery Plus Level 3 presents two types of regular reading selections: main stories and comprehension passages. Virtually all regular lessons and checkout lessons have a main story. Not all of these lessons have a comprehension passage. During the first half of the program, a comprehension passage appears in almost every regular lesson and checkout lesson. In the second half of the program, comprehension passages are less frequent, occurring in about half the lessons.

A list of comprehension passages and main stories appears by lesson in Appendix F.

Comprehension Passages

Comprehension passages are designed to prepare students for comprehending details of upcoming main stories. If a story contains information that students probably do not know, a comprehension passage precedes the main story. The comprehension passage is not as long as the main story, usually between 100 and 200 words. For example, a main story may refer to insects. Before students read this selection, they read a comprehension passage that gives them relevant information about insects.

If a comprehension passage appears in a lesson, it appears immediately before the reading of the main story. Here's the comprehension passage from lesson 41.

B
Insects

Most bugs are insects. Some bugs are not insects.

An ant is an insect. A fly is an insect. A butterfly is an insect. A beetle, a bee, and a grasshopper are insects. Spiders are not insects.

Here are the rules about all insects:
- An insect has six legs.
- The body of an insect has three parts.

An ant has six legs. Its body has three parts. So an ant is an insect.

A fly has six legs. Its body has three parts. So a fly is an insect.

A spider has eight legs. Its body has two parts. So a spider is not an insect.

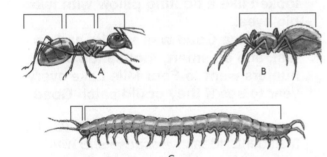

Main Stories

General Information

For main stories a word-decoding error limit is specified. The error limit for all main stories is based on two errors for each 100 words read aloud. The limits are designed so that students won't become anxious about reading and thus read hesitantly. At the same time, if students perform within the accuracy limits, they are accurately reading 98 out of 100 words.

The procedures for directing the reading of the story are spelled out in detail in the presentation book. Here is the format from lesson 15:

STORY READING

a. Find part C in your textbook. ✓
- We're going to read this story two times. First you'll read it out loud and make no more than 6 errors. Then I'll read it and ask questions.
b. Everybody, touch the title. ✓
- (Call on a student to read the title.) *[Goad the Toad.]*
- Everybody, what's the title? (Signal.) *Goad the Toad.*
c. (Call on individual students to read the story, each student reading two or three sentences at a time.)

- (Correct errors: Tell the word. Direct the student to reread the sentence.)
- (If the group makes more than 6 errors, direct the students to reread the story.)

d. (After the group has read the selection making no more than 6 errors:)
Now I'll read the story and ask questions.

Goad the Toad

Once there was a toad named Goad. Goad was the biggest toad you have ever seen. Goad was bigger than a baseball. She was even bigger than a toaster.

- Everybody, show me with your hands how big a toaster is. ✓
- Are there really toads that big? (Signal.) *No.*
- Real toads are about as big as my fist. So is Goad a real toad or a make-believe toad? (Signal.) *Make-believe toad.*

Goad was not only big. She was smart. She was smarter than a trained seal. Not only was Goad big and smart, Goad was fast. She was faster than a cat chasing a mouse.

- We know three things about Goad. Let me read that part again. You listen and get ready to tell the three things:
  Goad was not only big. She was smart. She was smarter than a trained seal. Not only was Goad big and smart, Goad was fast. She was faster than a cat chasing a mouse.
- Everybody, Goad was big and smart and what else? (Signal.) *Fast.*

Goad lived near a large lake called Four Mile Lake. It was four miles from one end of the lake to the other.

- Why was it called Four Mile Lake? (Call on a student. Idea: *Because it was four miles from one end to the other.*)
- The map shows Four Mile Lake. Touch the west bank of the lake. ✓
- There's a dotted line that goes through the lake. Follow that line and see how many miles you go before you reach the east bank. ✓
- Everybody, how many miles? (Signal.) *Four.*

Goad liked to visit places on Four Mile Lake. Sometimes, she would hop over to the logs near the north shore of the lake.

- Everybody, touch the letter at the north shore of the lake in the picture. ✓
- What letter? (Signal.) *T.*

Sometimes, she would hop over the hills on the south shore.

- Everybody, touch the letter at the south shore of the lake. ✓
- What letter? (Signal.) *B.*

Sometimes, she would go for a dip near the east shore of the lake.

- Everybody, touch the letter at the east shore of the lake. ✓
- What letter? (Signal.) *W.*

When Goad was in the water, she was not fast. She could not swim as fast as a seal or a goldfish. In fact, she could not swim as fast as a very slow frog.

- Everybody, was Goad fast on land? (Signal.) *Yes.*
- Was she fast in water? (Signal.) *No.*

**When Goad was in the water, she looked like a floating pillow with two big eyes.
Because Goad was so big, and so fast, and so smart, thousands of hunters went to Four Mile Lake every year to see if they could catch Goad.**

- Why did they want to catch her? (Call on a student. Ideas: *Because she was different from the other toads; because she was so big, fast, and smart.*)

People from the circus knew that if they had Goad, they could put on a show that would bring thousands of people to the circus.

- Would a great big smart toad make a good circus act? (Call on a student. Idea: *Yes.*)

Hunters from zoos knew that people would come from all over to visit any zoo that had a toad like Goad. Some hunters came because they wanted to become rich.

- How could they become rich by catching Goad? (Call on a student. Ideas: *Make people pay to see her; sell her to the zoo.*)

> **Goad was worth thousands of dollars to anybody who could catch her. But nobody was able to catch her.**
> **MORE NEXT TIME**

- Why do you suppose that nobody was able to catch Goad? (Call on a student. Ideas: *She was too smart; she was too fast.*)

Overview of Story-Reading Procedures

The story-reading procedures change throughout the program. Here is a summary of the procedures.

Lessons 1–91: On the first reading, students read the **entire** story aloud. You call on individual students, each to read two or three sentences. You may ask some comprehension questions. These usually relate to predictions about what will happen in the story. On the second reading, **you** read the entire story and ask the remaining comprehension items.

Lessons 92–145: On the first reading, students read most of the story aloud. They do not read the last part of the story, however. You present some comprehension items. On the second reading, you read the same part of the story the students have read. You present comprehension items that relate to this part. Then students read the end of the story to themselves, and you present comprehension items for that part.

Presenting Reading of Comprehension Passage and Main Story

Here are procedures for effectively directing the group reading of comprehension passages and main stories:

Make sure you receive a good sample of each student's reading behavior. For groups that have over 15 students, you may not receive adequate feedback about the performance of some students. The simplest remedy is to observe students reading individually during paired practice.

Make sure that students follow along as others are reading. Students are to point to the words that are being read. Pointing is a behavioral indication that those students who are not reading aloud are reading silently. Think of the pointing behavior as a way of maximizing practice. By pointing, the students practice reading throughout the group reading. If they don't point, they may practice only when they are reading aloud—a very scant amount of practice.

To ensure that students follow along, establish the procedure that students lose their turn if they don't have their place when they're called on.

If the group is large (over 15), circulate among the students and observe them from behind.

Decoding Errors in Main Stories

Each main story has an error limit. If students are placed appropriately, the group should regularly read within the error limit. Follow these guidelines for dealing with decoding errors:

Remind students of the error limit for the story and tell them how they are doing. Remember, we aren't going to make more than seven errors, so read carefully. Reinforce accurate reading: Good job. You're reading very carefully. Warn the students if they tend to make careless mistakes: The group has already made five errors, so be careful.

- If the students read within the error limit, congratulate them for doing a good job. Remind them that it is very hard: That was a tough story and this group read it making only __ errors. That's pretty good.

- If the students do not read within the error limit, (1) they are to reread the story, and (2) *you will ask no questions during this rereading.*

Try to schedule the rereading as soon as possible. If there is time in the period, start the rereading immediately. Typically, however, the rereading will have to be scheduled during the next reading lesson.

Tally each error and give immediate feedback. Here is a list of common decoding errors:

- *Omitting an ending.* Saying "look" for *looked* is an error. Saying "run" for *runs* is an error.

- *Saying the wrong word.* Saying "a" for *the* is an error. Saying "what" for *that* is an error.

- *Repeated self-corrections.* A self-correction occurs when a student says the wrong word and then rereads the word correctly before

you correct the student. If a student responds with the correct word after some signal has been given that the initial reading was wrong, count the self-correction as an error. If a student does a lot of self-correcting, count all self-corrections as errors. However, if the group makes only occasional self-corrections (no more than 1–3 per story), do not count them as errors.

- *Word omissions or insertions.* If a student reads *They went with the boys from town,* as "They went with the boys from **the** town," count the inserted word as an error. If a student reads the sentence as, "They went with boys from town," the omitted word should be counted as an error.

- *Repeated line skipping.* Like self-corrections, occasional line-skipping should not be treated as an error; simply tell the student to move up to the appropriate line and reread the entire sentence. However, if line-skipping occurs frequently, count each occurrence as one error.

- *Repeated partial readings.* If a student usually reads sentences in this manner: "They went with went with the boys from town," count one error. Occasional rereadings to fix the phrasing of the sentence are acceptable. Chronic rereadings, however, should be treated as errors.

- *Repeated word-part or syllable reading.* If a student usually pronounces longer words a part at a time before saying the word, the student is making decoding errors. Count each **chronic** occurrence of word-part or syllable reading as one error. For example, if the student reads "Ma—manu—manufac—manufacture," count one error.

Remember, the number of decoding errors will drop if you:

- give the students feedback on how they are doing.

- make sure that you are not letting errors pass.

- respond immediately to mistakes.

Correcting Decoding Errors During Selection Reading

There is only one procedure for correcting decoding errors during selection reading:

1. Stop the reader as soon as you hear the error.

2. Indicate whether the reader skipped a line, reread a word, omitted a word, or misread a word. For misread words, say the word and ask the student to repeat it: That word is _____. What word?

3. Direct the student to read the sentence from the beginning: Go back to the beginning of that sentence and read it again.

The last step is particularly important. The only way you know whether the correction was effectively communicated is that the student correctly reads the sentence in which the mistake occurred.

Recording Performance

The reproducible group summary chart that appears in Appendix H is designed for keeping track of:

- the group's performance on the reading of the main story;

- the performance of individual students on their five-lesson reading checkouts;

- students' tenth-lesson test performance;

- students' independent work.

Each chart covers a ten-lesson span. The sample chart on the next page has been partially filled in for lessons 41 to 50.

The top of the chart provides the summary information for the group. You record the number of errors the group made in reading each main story. If the group exceeds the error limit, you circle the number. The 9 for lesson 45 is circled because the error limit for lesson 45 is 8.

Presenting Comprehension Activities

The presentation script for each main story and comprehension passage indicates the comprehension items you are to present.

Present items specified for the first reading and the second reading. Comprehension passages are read once, but most main stories are read twice. The text indicates both the items that are to be presented on each reading and when they are to be presented.

Teacher **Ms. Turner**   *Reading Mastery Plus Level 3*   Group **2**

Lessons	4 1	4 2	4 3	4 4	CO 4 5	4 6	4 7	4 8	4 9	CO/Test 5	
Main Story Errors	7	8	8	8	(9)	11	7	5	9		
Name	IW	IW	IW	IW	CO	IW	IW	IW	IW	IW	CO	Test
Luis Cepeda					/						/	
Yoko Higashi					/						/	
Anita Diaz					/						/	
Denise Barton					/						/	
Zachary Gray					/						/	
Eric Adler					/						/	
					/						/	

Items that are to be presented on the first (or only) reading are preceded by a small number 1.

Items that are preceded by a small number 2 are to be presented on the second reading. These appear only in the script for the main stories (not for comprehension passages, because there is no second reading for comprehension passages). All second-reading items are preceded by a small number 2.

The following sample is from lesson 119. The boldface text is the story the students read. After Toby says to himself, "What a shabby circus," on the first reading, you say, If it's a shabby circus, does it have a lot of good acts? After students read what Toby said to himself during the second reading, you do not present a comprehension item.

Some of the illustrations are reproduced in the script, and items immediately follow the illustration. For example, the script shows an illustration and some questions following the second reading of the sentence, "The rest of them were complaining." The items below the illustration refer to the illustration.

STORY READING

a. Find part C in your textbook. ✓
- The error limit for group reading is 10. Read carefully.

b. Everybody, touch the title. ✓
- (Call on a student to read the title.) [*Toby's New Job.*]
- Everybody, what's the title? (Signal.) *Toby's New Job.*
- Where did we leave Toby? (Call on a student. Idea: *In his cage at the circus.*)
- What time of day was it? (Call on a student. Idea: *Nighttime.*)
- How did Toby feel? (Call on a student. Ideas: *Sad; homesick.*)

c. (Call on individual students to read the story, each student reading two or three sentences at a time. Ask questions marked **1.**)

- (Correct errors: Tell the word. Direct the student to reread the sentence.)
- (If the group makes more than 10 errors, direct the students to reread the story.)

d. (After the group has read the selection making no more than 10 errors, read the story to the students and ask questions marked **2.**)

Toby's New Job

The next morning, the circus owner came and took Toby from his cage. The owner said, "You are going to do tricks for the people who have come to see our circus. If you want to eat, you will do tricks. If you do **not** do tricks, you will become a **very** hungry animal."

Toby said, "Oh, bad and super bad."

1. Why would Toby become a very hungry animal if he does not do tricks? (Call on a student. Idea: *Because the circus owner wouldn't feed him.*)

1. Do you think he'll do tricks for the circus owner? (Call on individual students. Student preference.)

The owner took Toby into a tent. In the middle of the tent was a ring.

"What a shabby circus," Toby said to himself.

1. If it's a shabby circus, does it have a lot of good acts? (Signal.) *No.*

This circus did not have many animals and people doing super things. Toby was the only animal in the tent. The owner was dressed up in a black suit with a rip in the back of the coat.

There was no huge crowd of people watching the act. There were about twenty people sitting in the stands. Three of them were sleeping. Two of them were little kids who were crying. The rest of them were complaining.

2. The picture on the next page shows the shabby circus.

2. Touch the circus owner. ✓

2. Look at the rip in the back of his suit.

2. Everybody, about how many people are in the stands? (Signal.) *20.*

2. Touch somebody who is sleeping. ✓

One girl said, "We want to see lions and tigers."

"Yeah," somebody else said. "We don't want to see a dumb kangaroo."

> The owner held up his hands. "This kangaroo can do tricks that will surprise you. This kangaroo is the smartest kangaroo in the world. People usually pay as much as a hundred dollars to see this kangaroo perform."

2. Everybody, is the circus owner telling the truth? (Signal.) *No.*

> "Boo," the people yelled. "We want lions."
> Then a girl yelled, "Make that kangaroo ride a bicycle."
> "Make him ride it backward," a boy yelled.
> The other people began to clap. "Yes, let's see him ride a bicycle backward."
> "Wouldn't you rather see him being shot from a cannon?" the owner asked.
> "No," the people agreed. "We want to see that kangaroo ride a bicycle backward."
> The owner tried to argue with the crowd, but when people started to throw things at him, he said, "All right, he will ride a bicycle backward."

2. At first the circus owner argued with the crowd. What did he want to do to Toby? (Call on a student. Idea: *Shoot him from a cannon.*)
2. Everybody, did the crowd agree with the circus owner? (Signal.) *No.*
2. So did the circus owner finally agree to have Toby ride a bicycle backward? (Signal.) *Yes.*

> The owner got a dusty bicycle. He held up one hand and said to the crowd, "Ladies and gentlemen. Today the Kankan Circus presents Toby, the wonder kangaroo. Toby will amaze you by riding a bicycle backward. And he will do this

> backward. And he will do this amazing trick on a high wire ten meters above the floor."

2. Where is Toby supposed to ride the bicycle? (Call on a student. Idea: *On a high wire 10 meters above the floor.*)

> Toby looked up at the wire ten meters above the floor. You know what Toby said.

1. Say what he probably said. (Call on a student. Idea: *Oh, double bad.*)

> The owner handed Toby the bicycle and said, "Take this bicycle up the ladder. Then ride it backward on the high wire."
> Toby shook his head, no.
> The owner said, "<u>Do</u> it, you bad kangaroo. Get up there and ride that bicycle."
> Toby shook his head, no.
> The owner turned to the crowd. "Before Toby, the wonder kangaroo, rides the bicycle on the high wire, he will ride it backward on the floor."

2. The circus owner changed the announcement because Toby wouldn't do it on the high wire.

> The owner turned to Toby. "Ride that bicycle on the floor."
> Toby shook his head, no.
> People were beginning to throw things at Toby and the owner. "This is a rip-off," they were hollering. "That kangaroo can't do anything."
> The owner said, "One moment, ladies and gentlemen. Before Toby rides the bicycle backward on the floor, Toby will ride it forward on the floor."
> The owner looked at Toby and said, "Do it." Toby shook his head, no.

> **People were now yelling, "I want my money back," and "Let's call a cop."**

1. Go back to the beginning of the story. Follow along while I read.

2. What was the last thing the owner wanted Toby to do? (Signal.) *Ride the bicycle forward on the floor.*

2. Is it easier to ride **forward** or **backward?** (Signal.) *Forward.*

2. Read the rest of the story to yourself. Find out two things. First find out what Toby was supposed to do before he rode the bicycle forward on the floor. Then find out what two boys in the crowd did. Raise your hand when you're done.

> **The owner held up his hands and said, "Before Toby rides the bicycle forward on the floor, Toby will walk with the bicycle on the floor."**
>
> **Toby looked at the owner and shook his head no again.**
>
> **"This is the worst show in the world," people were yelling. A woman was shaking her umbrella at the owner. Two boys were throwing papers at Toby. Toby was saying, "Oh, worse than bad."**

2. (After all students have raised their hand:) What was Toby supposed to do before he rode the bicycle forward on the floor? (Call on a student. Idea: *Walk with the bicycle on the floor.*)

2. Everybody, is he going to do that? (Signal.) *No.*

2. What were two boys in the crowd doing? (Call on a student. Idea: *Throwing papers at Toby.*)

2. Raise your hand if you remember what Toby said as the boys threw papers at him. (Call on a student.) *[Oh, worse than bad.]*

2. That must be the worst circus in the world.

Do not become sidetracked into long discussions. Certainly you may present additional tasks; however, these should be infrequent. For example, if the students have had problems with a particular name or concept, it's all right to add a task even though the script does not indicate an item. If a specified task asks for student opinions, do not poll the entire group. A couple of quick responses will suffice.

Use the wording indicated in the script. Tasks that begin with the word *everybody* call for a group, unison response. Tasks that say *Call on a student* are to be presented to a single student. Tasks that are followed by *Call on individual students* call for a range of responses. In some cases, the task will call for an opinion, such as: What do you think will happen? In other cases, the students are asked to name items that fall into a particular category: Name some animals that are warm-blooded.

Accept appropriate ideas for tasks that are answered by an individual. The appropriate response for the first task (Where did we leave Toby?) is expressed as an idea. (Idea: *In his cage at the circus.*) An appropriate response is one that clearly expresses this **idea,** regardless of the specific words used in the response— *at a shabby circus, in a run-down circus.* Present a follow-up task if the response is not sufficiently specific. For example, if a student responds "in a cage," you would say, Where was that cage?

Use a real globe of the world to present those tasks that specify a globe. These tasks appear in lessons 39, 46–48, 51, 113, 132, 135, and 139. Make sure that you have a globe available. Do not try to use a flat map instead of a globe. The concepts that are conveyed through the presentation of the globe are critical. If you don't present them as specified, a large percentage of students will not learn these concepts and will fail a host of review items that assume a basic understanding of the globe.

Reducing Comprehension Errors

If the students make a mistake on an oral comprehension task, correct the error, mark the task, and tell them: I'm going to ask that question later. So remember the answer. At the end of the story, present any marked tasks. If an individual turn was missed, present the task to an individual (not necessarily the same one who missed the task).

Correcting Comprehension Errors During Selection Reading

You will correct two types of tasks: tasks in which students have just read the passage that answers the questions and tasks in which the information was presented earlier.

For each type of correction, you will follow this general pattern:

1. Make sure students have the information they need to answer the question.

2. Repeat the task.

3. Repeat the task again at a later time.

For different item types, there are corresponding variations of this correction.

- If the passage the students just read answers the question, reread the passage or summarize the content before repeating the task the students missed.

- If the passage students just read does not answer the question, you will tell the students the information they need to answer the question before you repeat the task.

- If the passage does not give the answer and if further facts will not clarify the answer, you tell them the answer, then repeat the task.

When information is presented in the passage students just read, you make sure they have the information they need either by rereading the passage or by telling them the relevant information. Sometimes, you'll be able to give them the information they need by asking them a series of questions. If you can't think of good questions to ask, however, you can simply tell them the information they need.

Example: Why would Toby become a very hungry animal if he does not do tricks? A student responds, *"He wouldn't eat enough,"* which is possibly correct. You ask, But why wouldn't he eat enough? The student fails to answer.

1. **Repeat the part that answers the question:** Listen to that part again: The owner said, "You are going to do tricks for the people who have come to see our circus. If you want to eat, you will do tricks. If you do not do tricks, you will become a very hungry animal."

2. Repeat the task: Why would Toby become a very hungry animal if he does not do tricks?

3. Give the correct answer, if necessary: If the student doesn't respond appropriately, say, The **owner** wouldn't feed him.

4. Remind the students that you'll repeat the task at a later time: Remember that answer. I'm going to ask the question later. At a later time, repeat the question.

When not all information is presented in the passage students just read, you tell students the information they need.

Here's the correction for a mistake from lesson 117. The item involves knowledge of Pip's show-off behavior.

Example: Why would Pip like to stand in the bright sun? The student responds, "I don't know."

1. Refer to information presented earlier: Does Pip think he is beautiful? *Yes.*

Can people see how beautiful he is if there's not much light? *No.*

2. Repeat the task: Why would Pip like to stand in the bright sun?

3. Give the correct answer, if necessary: Because the sunlight will show off his feathers.

4. Repeat the task at a later time.

At the end of the period, or at another time the group members are present (after recess, just before lunch, etc.) ask the students questions they missed. Remember to give them enough story information for them to answer the question.

When additional facts do not clarify the answer:

1. Tell students the answer.

2. Repeat the task.

3. Repeat the task at a later time.

Note that these items usually ask "Why?" or require students to make a judgment or draw a conclusion. Here's an example from lesson 117: Why would the sailors want to hide the animals? A student responds, "*I don't know.*"

Here's the correction:

1. Tell the student the answer: They don't want the police to know that they have animals like peacocks and kangaroos on the ship.

2. Repeat the original task: Why would the sailors want to hide the animals?

3. Remind the students that you'll repeat the task at a later time.

Correcting Errors on Picture Tasks

Some picture tasks require students to touch an illustration or operate on it in some way. The task may be, Touch that path, or Touch the steam rising from the pond. These tasks are presented to the group, but are not accompanied by a signal to respond. Responses are incorrect if students:

- copy responses produced by a neighbor

- touch the wrong object

- fail to respond

- give ambiguous responses

To correct picture mistakes, show the students the right response. If possible, repeat the task later.

Example: The picture shows objects being drawn to a whirlpool. The task is: Touch object C and trace the path it will take. The mistake: A student points in a vague manner above the page or does not clearly trace the path. The correction: Put your finger right on the page. Touch point C. Now follow the dotted line and show me the way the object will move. Do not accept ambiguous responses.

Some picture tasks require students to observe details of pictures and produce **verbal** responses about these details. Treat these verbal responses the same way you would treat responses to a written question. The picture answers the question you ask, so you would tell students the answer, repeat the task, and possibly repeat it later (although it may be difficult to do this without the book).

Here's an example from lesson 39.

What is C? *Copilot.*

Correction:

1. **You tell the answer:** It's a flight attendant.

2. **You repeat the task:** What is C?

3. **Later you can ask students a question that is like the one you presented.**

Paired Practice

General Information

Following the main-story reading, students work in pairs and reread part of the story. Each student reads about 200 words. Students are permanently assigned. Partners are to sit next to each other. They can either read from the same text or from two texts. Allow 5 minutes for paired practice.

Possible Problems

Here are the more common problems teachers encounter when implementing paired-practice procedures:

1. Students take too long to get started.

2. Students take too long to complete the reading.

3. Students become lax about following along when they are not reading and therefore do not respond to the partner's errors.

For problem 1: The simplest way to get students into the reading faster is to have a structured beginning. One good plan is to require some sort of response for the pair—such as both partners sitting next to each other with books in place and raising their hands. They are not to start reading until you acknowledge that they have raised their hands.

It's time for paired practice. Raise your hand when you and your partner are ready.

Acknowledge each pair and tell them to start.

Praise students who start quickly, That was a good start. Almost all the teams are ready to read.

If some partners consistently take more than a few seconds to get ready for the paired practice, reassign the members of the team, or place a stronger contingency on getting started on time.

For problem 2: Set up a reinforcing contingency for completing the reading in a reasonable amount of time. If students often take 8 minutes to complete the reading, set the time limit at 7 minutes and give students who perform within this time limit praise and possibly some other reinforcer. After students consistently read within 7 minutes, change the time limit to 6 minutes.

For problem 3: Monitor the students as they read and have students report on their partner's errors.

If students are not catching errors their partners make, require the checker to write the number of errors the partner made.

At the end of the paired practice, record a quick summary:

A team, raise your hand if your partner made no errors.

Raise your hand if your partner made 1 or 2 errors.

Raise your hand if your partner made more than two errors.

Summarize the results on the board. Then conclude, Well, it looks like the B team won today, but not by much. We'll see who wins next time.

The system works because the students want their team to win. If students miss their partner's errors, however, the partner's team gets an advantage.

Independent Work

General Information

As part of every lesson, the students work independently for about 20 to 30 minutes, completing all the textbook items specified for that lesson as well as completing side 1 and side 2 of that lesson's worksheet.

Here are the types of items students work:

- Items based on the comprehension passage read that day (only on lessons that have a comprehension passage);

- Items based on the main story in the lesson;

- Skill items (sequencing, deductions, vocabulary review, alphabetizing, etc.);

- Review items based on information from earlier lessons (either from comprehension passages or main stories);

In addition, students independently write sentences. This work is part of a 10-minute, writing-spelling period that occurs at another time of day. (See **Writing and Spelling Lessons,** page 73.)

Early Preparation

During the first part of the program, the teacher reads the items.

- Lessons 1–5. The teacher reads all independent work items aloud. After reading each item, the teacher calls on a student to answer the item. The teacher corrects mistakes and repeats items that students miss.

- Lessons 6–9. After the main story, individual students read and answer all items except review items.

- Lessons 11–15. After the main story, students orally read items for the comprehension passage and the main story but do not answer them aloud. The teacher introduces new types of skill items.

- Lessons 16–35. After the main story, students orally read only the main-story items. The teacher continues to introduce new types of skill items.

- Lessons 36–145. As a rule some items appear in the textbook and some on the worksheets. The teacher does not read items, with the exception of specific skill items. When new types of skill items are introduced, the teacher goes over them with the students.

Observe Students as They Work Independently

Plan to observe the group at work on the independent-work activities every few lessons, especially during the first 20 lessons.

Identify specific problems students have. Make sure they are on task and are not copying from each other. Serious problems should be corrected immediately.

Is the student reading items correctly?
As part of answering correctly, students must read items correctly. Often it is possible to infer how a student misread an item from the response. For example, an item reads, "Why was Toby happy when he saw the police boat?" The student answers, "Yes." Inference: The student read the item as "Was Toby happy when he saw the police boat?" Tell the student: I don't think you read that item carefully. Read it again.

Note: As a rule, you shouldn't help a student more than once during a lesson. The more you help, the less information you have about what a student actually knows, and the more the student will rely on you for help.

Is the student working at a reasonable rate? Students who are just learning how to work independently often don't use their time well. They need feedback about how much time has passed and how they are performing.

A good tactic is to remind the students about their rate of performance. As you observe different students, make positive comments to the group about different students' rates: Oh, here's somebody who's already finished the workbook items. Very good . . . Here's somebody else who is almost that far along. Fantastic.

If the students tend to go slowly, make sure you give students feedback about how they are doing as they work. For example, after they have worked for about fifteen minutes, remind them that they should have finished about half the independent work assignment.

Help students who get "stuck" on a particular item. They may not have a strategy for completing the exercises and then returning to problem items. Explain the strategy of (1) circling the number of a problem item, (2) skipping that item and working all non-problem items, and (3) returning to the problem (circled) item.

Are the answers to items correct? Refer to the answer key. If the answer a student wrote is not correct, tell the student something like: Your answer to item 5 is not correct. You should not tell the student the answer, and usually you should not provide more than one of these prompts to each student per lesson.

Answers that are obviously correct present no problem. But you may have questions about answers that have grammatical errors, that do not correspond precisely to the answer given in the answer key, or that contain misspelled words.

Some of the answers in the key are labeled "Idea." This designation means that the student's response must give a correct answer; however, the students are not required to use the exact words that appear in the key. The reason these items are shown as having "idea" answers is that there are different ways of expressing the answer, and all answers that express the idea are equally correct.

Here's an item with some responses that students wrote. Item: Why did the Vikings like Tom and Eric's dog?

In the selection, their dog growled at a woman, and defeated the Viking's best dog.

Below is the answer key for this item:

11. Why did the Vikings like Tom and Eric's dog?

Ideas: Because it was a good fighter; because it was mean.

A response that expresses **either** of these ideas would be correct. Below are responses students wrote. Some of these answers are clearly correct or incorrect. Others present problems. You can test the items by asking yourself, Do I know what the student is trying to say? Did the student use enough words to really say that? Can I overlook any wording misuse and still judge that the student expressed the idea?

1. *He won their best dog.* Clearly, the student means he **beat** their best dog. The problem is usage. The student expressed the idea. The answer is correct.

2. *It beat the other dog.* This answer has no problems. It clearly expresses the idea and uses adequate wording.

3. *To fight with dogs.* The answer is wrong. It does not answer the question: Why did the Vikings like their dog? Furthermore, the item does not express the idea that their dog won the fight.

4. *It fought the dog.* The answer is probably wrong, but you might give it the benefit of the doubt. The Vikings were impressed by the skill of the dog, not by the mere fact that it fought. However, you could argue that it takes courage to fight.

5. *It was mad.* The answer is clearly wrong. The student may be trying to say, "It was mean," but **mad** and **mean** are not close enough, and we can't overlook the difference because the word **mad** is the only clue we have about what the student is trying to say.

6. *It was fast.* The answer is clearly wrong. (The story mentioned that the dogs were the same size but that Tom and Eric's dog was faster. However, the story gave no indication that the Vikings were impressed by the speed, but rather by the victory.)

7. *It did not stop.* The answer is wrong.

Do students spell the words correctly? Here are some rules about spelling errors for **words that are not spelling words:**

1. If the word appears in the item, it should be spelled correctly in the answer.

2. If the word does not appear in the item, it will not be counted wrong if it is spelled incorrectly.

If *down* is a spelling word, the students could be held accountable for it. However, don't try to identify every spelling word students should know. Spot-check items as you monitor the students. If you notice spelling words that are misspelled, mark them, but focus primarily on the words in the item. If the answers have words that appear in the item, the words should be spelled correctly.

Are the answers to *how* and *why* questions expressed appropriately? Some students do not write appropriate answers to these questions. For instance, the item, "Why did he go to the library?" is appropriately answered, "To get a book," or

"Because he wanted a book," or "He wanted a book." Some students, however, may write, "A book." That answer is unacceptable.

To correct this type of response, present items orally. Then direct students to write appropriate answers.

Note that when students answer the questions orally, they tend to answer them correctly. For example:

Listen: Why did he go to the library?

To get a book.

Yes, **to get a book.** Those are the words that answer the question. Say those words.

To get a book.

Write them.

Present tasks like the previous one until students are very firm on the words they are to write.

Remedies for students who can't remember story information. Starting with lesson 36, the basic procedure is for students to complete their independent work without first hearing items read or answered. Students are supposed to remember the information from reading the story and answering the oral comprehension items (which usually include all the written items they will respond to).

If some students have great difficulty remembering the information from the story and continue to make mistakes on independent work because they don't recall the answers, you may introduce a temporary procedure:

• Direct students who have problems

remembering the information to write answers to all the items they can work.

• Next, have them circle the number of any items they cannot answer.

• Direct them to read these items to themselves.

• Tell them, Remember the questions that are circled because you'll look in your story to find the answers.

• Permit them to look at their story one time to find answers to all items. Students are not to write anything during the time they are looking in the story. Also, students are to limit their information search to the lesson that was read today. They are not to refer to earlier selections.

Pencils down. You may look at today's story one time to find answers you couldn't remember. You have three minutes. You have to find answers to all your questions in three minutes. You can't write anything until you're done reading.

• Monitor students and make sure that they do not write the answer to one question and then attempt to look at the story again. Remind them, You can only look at the story one time.

Repeat the procedure on no more than 12 lessons. Remind students that they should try to remember the answers when the story is being read by the group. Reinforce students who improve in remembering information.

Workchecks

General Information

The goal of the workcheck is to review the independent-work tasks and to make sure that (1) students are not making too many errors and (2) students learn the correct answers to items they miss. The workcheck is not mere paper marking. It is teaching. It is particularly important for *Reading Mastery Plus* Level 3 because many items will appear as review items on later lessons. Some students will miss these items repeatedly unless you present daily workchecks.

The independent work consists of the worksheet pages for the lesson and answers to textbook items written on lined paper.

During the workcheck, you go over all the items and students mark all items that are wrong.

At the end of the workcheck students record the total number of errors they made at the top of the lined paper. Students change all incorrect answers and hand in their lined paper and their worksheet (side 1 and side 2).

You quickly spot-check the worksheet answers and those on lined paper. Don't spot-check only items that had mistakes, because some students are not reliable about marking incorrect answers.

After the spot-check, you will use the Group Summary Chart to record the number of errors each student made on the lesson. (See **Recording Errors,** page 58.)

A "passing grade" for each lesson is three or fewer errors. This criterion is fairly stiff because many lessons call for 35–40 responses. The structure of the program makes it possible for most students to pass almost all lessons. The record of errors may be used to award grades. More importantly, the error performance indicates how well the students are performing, what they are mastering, and whether they need additional practice.

The workchecks are designed to provide that practice and to assure that students continue to perform well in the lessons.

A workcheck is most efficiently handled as a group activity. It should be conducted some time after the group has completed the independent work activities, but before the next lesson is presented.

Although details of the procedure may vary from situation to situation, here are things you should do during the daily workcheck:

- Check the written responses to all items. (Answer keys for worksheet and textbook items appear in the Answer Key book.)

- Make sure that all incorrect responses are marked with an **X.**

- Give the students information about correct answers to items, so they can later change their incorrect answers.

- Make a final check of each student's written work after the student has changed all the incorrect answers.

• Then record the number of errors (the number of items originally marked with an X and later corrected).

The workcheck should not take a great deal of time. In most cases, it requires only six to nine minutes. If it takes much longer, (a) your pacing is too slow, or (b) the students are not firm in some skills that are important in completing the independent work. Work on both possibilities.

Presenting Workchecks

Students may check their own independent work during the workcheck. They should use a colored pencil for checking.

The fastest procedure for going through the workcheck is for you to **read each item and call on a student to tell the correct answer.** Students who have questions may raise their hand. If many students have questions about a particular item, tell them to mark the item with a question mark. Go quickly to the next item.

As you read the items and give the answers, circulate among the students. Make sure they are marking each incorrect response with an **X.** By circulating among the students, you will discourage the students' tendency to change their answers without first marking the item as incorrect.

Firm items that a lot of students tend to miss, and firm students who consistently make more than three errors on their independent work. You firm by giving additional practice.

There are different formats for firming, but the simplest is for you to go over the items

that many students miss and provide paired practice for students who tend to make too many errors.

For example, some students tend to have trouble with measurement units—inch, centimeter, meter, yard. Plan to firm the group by having them use their hands to show you an inch, a yard, etc. Take a minute or two at the end of the workcheck and present the task, Everybody, show me a space that is about an inch . . . Show me a space that is about a meter and so forth. If students tend to copy the responses of others, direct them to keep their eyes closed during the tasks. Close your eyes and show me a space that is about a foot . . . Open your eyes. You should have a space about this wide . . .

Don't try to firm all difficult items in one setting. Instead, give students short bursts of practice (10–15 trials) in possibly three or four lessons.

For students who consistently make three or more errors, provide paired practice. Pair the lower students with students who do well on the independent work. The higher student presents the various items the other student missed and gives feedback on each answer. The paired practice could be scheduled for about five minutes a lesson (possibly at the end of the workcheck period).

Plan to firm students on sets of related facts—particularly geographic information and time-line information. In both cases, some students confuse similar facts. (Students are often naive about dates; however, they are required to learn quite a few dates.)

The simplest format is like the fact-review, a sample of which appears below.

FACT REVIEW

a. Let's review some facts you have learned.
    First we'll go over the facts together.
    Then I'll call on different students to do some facts.

b. Everybody, tell me when Eric and Tom were in the Land of the Vikings.
    (Pause.) Get ready. (Signal.) *1000.*
    • Tell me when Eric and Tom were in San Francisco. (Pause.) Get ready. (Signal.) *1906.*
    • Tell me when Eric and Tom were in the city of the future. (Pause.) Get ready. (Signal.) *4000 years in the future.*
    • Tell me when the United States became a country. (Pause.) Get ready. (Signal.) *1776.*
    • (Repeat step b until firm.)

c. Tell me when Greece and Troy went to war. (Pause.) Get ready. (Signal.) *3000 years ago.*
    • Tell me when Eric and Tom were in Egypt. (Pause.) Get ready. (Signal.) *5000 years ago.*
    • Tell me when Columbus discovered America. (Pause.) Get ready. (Signal.) *1492.*
    • Tell me when Eric and Tom were in Concord. (Pause.) Get ready. (Signal.) *1777.*
    • (Repeat step c until firm.)

Individual Test
• Now I'm going to call on each of you to do some facts. (Call on each student to do the facts in one step.)

The review consists of three or four items that students tend to confuse and two or three items that generally give students no trouble.

You may use this format for geography items, measurement items, or any group of items that students tend to confuse.

If students make a lot of mistakes on independent work, direct them to redo either the entire page on which the errors occurred, or just the part that presented problems.

Recording Errors

Record errors for independent work for the students *after* you have looked at their corrected work. The number of independent-work errors has been written by the students at the top of the lined paper (at the end of the workcheck). Check the numbers for accuracy. Record the number of errors in column **IW** of your Group Summary Chart.

The sample Group Summary Chart on the next page has been filled out for lessons 41 through 49. The shaded areas show the parts of the chart used for recording independent-work errors.

A passing grade for each lesson is three or fewer errors. Yoko Higashi's **IW** performance for lesson 41 is circled, indicating that a remedy is needed.

It is important to monitor students' independent work performance. If students start making a large number of errors on their independent work, firm them before proceeding in the program.

Teacher Ms. Turner   **Group** 2

Lessons	41	42	43	44	CO 45		46	47	48	49	CO/Test 5	
Main Story Errors	7	8	8	8		(9)	11	7	5	9		
Name	IW	IW	IW	IW	CO	IW	IW	IW	IW	IW	CO	Test
Luis Cepeda	2	1	2	1	/	2	1	0	1	3	/	
Yoko Higashi	(4)	3	2	2	/	2	3	1	2	2	/	
Anita Diaz	1	1	1	0	/	2	1	1	0	2	/	
Denise Barton	1	2	0	1	/	1	0	1	0	2	/	
Zachary Gray	1	0	0	1	/	1	2	1	1	1	/	
Eric Adler	2	1	1	0	/	1	0	1	0	2	/	
					/						/	

Individual Reading Checkouts

General Information

During every fifth lesson, starting with lesson 10, each student receives an individual reading checkout. In these lessons that end with the digit 5 (15, 25, etc.), the paired practice is deleted. Students therefore have time for the individual checkouts. The average time available for individual reading checkouts is about fifteen minutes.

Checkouts take about a minute-and-a-half per student. If the group is large, you may need an additional checker. You may use an aide, an older student, a parent volunteer, or possibly a higher-performing student in the classroom. The main qualification for a checker is the ability

to identify reading errors and keep accurate time. If an additional checker is not available, you may be able to finish the checkouts at some later time in the school day. Possibly, you could finish them during the next lesson.

Each checkout is conducted by an aide, adult volunteer, or by the teacher.

To conduct checkouts, the checker calls up individual students as the group works on independent-work activities. The student orally reads a specified passage from the main story of the preceding lesson. For example, for the checkout in lesson 30, each student reads a specified passage from lesson 29. The passage in the student textbook has marks at the beginning and at the end (✿).

The checker times each student. **To pass the checkout, the student must read the**

passage in one minute or less and make no more than two errors.

Conducting Individual Reading Checkouts

Identify a part of the room where a student can read individually to you or to the assigned checker. The simplest procedure is for the checker to:

- Sit next to the student.

- Tell the student when to begin reading.

- Observe the text that the student reads.

- Make a tally mark on a sheet of paper for each error.

- Help if the student gets stuck on a word for more than two seconds.

- Record the time it takes the student to complete the passage.

Decoding errors consist of word misidentifications, word omissions, line-skipping, and word additions. (Self-corrects and rereading words also may be counted as errors. See page 41.)

Note that the checker is not to correct errors unless the correction is necessary for the student to keep reading the passage. If the student can't read a word within about two seconds, the checker says the word and marks it as an error. The checker may first ask, "Do you want me to tell you the word?"

Students' Records

Each student keeps a record of reading checkout performance with thermometer charts (reproducible copies of which are at the back of student workbooks and in Appendix J of this guide). During the program, the student will fill in three thermometer charts. Together, they show all the reading checkouts the student passed.

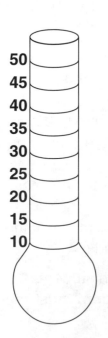

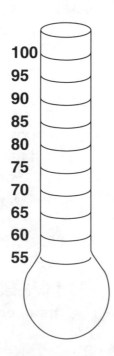

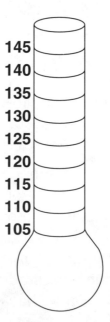

- The current thermometer charts may be posted in the classroom, kept in individual student folders, or in a central folder that you keep.

- If a student passes a checkout on the first trial, the student colors the appropriate space of the thermometer red. For example, if the student passes the checkout for lesson 35, the student colors the space for 35 red.

- If the student passes the checkout, but not on the first trial, the student colors the appropriate space, but not red. You may use blue, black, pink, or some other color.

   When the student completes *Reading Mastery Plus* Level 3, all three thermometer charts should be completely filled in. The colors show whether the student needed additional firming, and where that firming occurred.

Recording Rate-and-Accuracy Performance

Use column **CO** on the Group Summary Chart to record the number of errors each student made and whether the student passed (**P**) or failed (**F**) the rate criterion (one minute or less).

The **CO** columns on the Group Summary Chart have two parts. Record **P** or **F** in the top half of the box to indicate whether the student **passed** or **failed** the rate criterion. Record the student's number of decoding errors in the bottom half of the box.

The sample Group Summary Chart on page 62 has been filled out for lessons 41 through 50. The shaded columns show the parts of the chart used to record rate and accuracy performance for the individual reading checkouts in lesson 45 and lesson 50 (test 5). Note that Denise Barton's **CO** performance for lesson 45 is circled, indicating that a remedy is needed.

Firming Students Who Do Not Pass Checkouts

The students who do not pass a checkout on their first attempt should reread the passage aloud until they achieve an acceptable rate-accuracy performance. During these readings, students should be told which words they missed. After each reading, they should study the passage and then reread that passage to the checker.

Students who don't pass two consecutive attempts to meet the rate-accuracy criterion for a checkout should receive additional oral-reading practice.

- This practice should be modeled after the individual reading checkouts, with the exception that the student who is reading should receive immediate feedback about words that are misread. The checker simply tells the correct word.

- A plan that works well is to direct the student to read the last two or three stories that the group has read. Use the same error limit that is specified for group reading.

Teacher Ms. Turner   **Group** 2

Lessons	41	42	43	44	CO 45		46	47	48	49	CO/Test 5	
Main Story Errors	7	8	8	8	(9)		11	7	5	9		
Name	IW	IW	IW	IW	CO	IW	IW	IW	IW	IW	CO	Test
Luis Cepeda	2	1	2	1	P/0	2	1	0	1	3	P/0	
Yoko Higashi	(4)	3	2	2	P/0	2	3	1	2	2	P/1	
Anita Diaz	1	1	1	0	P/0	2	1	1	0	2	P/0	
Denise Barton	1	2	0	1	(F)/1	1	0	1	0	2	P/2	
Zachary Gray	1	0	0	1	P/0	1	2	1	1	1	P/0	
Eric Adler	2	1	1	0	P/1	1	0	1	0	2	P/1	

• Monitor the student's paired-reading practice. Make sure that the student is participating and the partner is responding to any mistakes the reader makes. If the practice is not adequate, either reassign the student to another partner or increase the amount of paired-reading practice the student receives.

Often, the student who is weak in decoding will tend to make a greater number of errors when tackling long passages. Therefore, the checker can take turns with the student, the checker reading one paragraph (or a few lines) and the student reading the next few lines.

A good variation is for the checker to read somewhat haltingly and make mistakes from time to time. The student is to catch these mistakes. By reading haltingly, the checker ensures that the student will be able to follow along. Requiring the student to catch the checker's mistakes ensures that the student is attending to the words even when not reading aloud. The periods during which the checker reads are therefore not merely "breaks." They are a switch from one kind of accuracy performance to another.

Fact Games

General Information

Fact games occur every tenth lesson as part of the test lessons, starting with lesson 30. The game is presented before the test. Fact games give students a great deal of practice with facts and rule applications. The games are important because many oral tasks presented during the regular lessons are answered by individuals, not by the whole group, which means that the students may not receive sufficient practice with many tasks.

Some facts are particularly troublesome for many students. The games provide intensive practice on these facts, but do so in a context that is reinforcing. The games become a combination of work and fun.

Groups of four players and a monitor play the game. (More than one group can play simultaneously.) Each group has a question sheet (or sheets) with 11 items numbered 2 through 12. The teacher reproduces these Fact Game sheets from blackline masters located in Appendix G.

To take a turn, a player rolls two dice (or number cubes). The player then adds the numbers on the cubes together, reads the item that corresponds to that number total (2 through 12), and responds to the item (which may involve answering several questions).

An assigned student monitor refers to the answer key in the back of the textbook and indicates whether the answer is correct. If so, the player earns a point and a checkmark is made on the student's scorecard. After 10 minutes, direct all students who earn more than 10 points to stand up.

On the next page is the fact game from lesson 90 and scorecard 90.

Reproducible Fact-Game scorecard sheets appear at the back of each workbook and at the back of this guide. Each student needs a copy for lessons 30 through 140.

Introducing the First Fact Game

The instructions for the first game (lesson 30) specify that you will be the monitor and demonstrate with four players how the game is played. When demonstrating the game, make sure that you model fast pacing, correct procedures, and appropriate responses to the players.

After demonstrating a few "rounds" of the game, assign students to permanent groups. Ideally, a group should consist of four players and a monitor. In some situations, you may have to form a group that consists of three or five players and a monitor. If possible, try to avoid larger groups. Each player in a larger group will receive fewer turns, and managing the group becomes more difficult.

Do not make groups homogeneous. (Do not place the better performers in one group and the lower performers in the other.) Rather, mix students of varying ability.

Assign monitors who are competent. The monitors should be good readers. Tell the monitors their responsibilities. They are to make sure that the players are taking turns, moving to the left. The monitor directs the player who is taking a turn to read the item aloud and answer it. Then the monitor confirms a correct response or gives the correct answer if the item was missed.

The next player does not roll the cubes until the preceding player has answered and has been told whether the response is correct. (If players are permitted to roll before the item is read and answered, they become so intent on getting ready for their turn that they do not listen to the preceding player's item and the answer.)

Fact Game

2. a. Which army was Achilles in during the war between Troy and Greece?

    b. How long was he in the war?

    c. Who won when he fought against Hector?

3. a. Who was the greatest soldier of Troy?

    b. Achilles rode around the wall of Troy in a ▬▬.

4. a. Name a good place to look for clues about people who lived long ago.

    b. Tell when eohippus lived.

5. As you touch each horse, say the letter. Then name the horse.

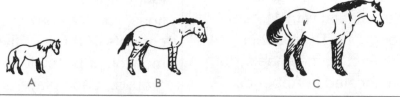

6. a. Things closer to the top of the pile went into the pile ▬▬.

    b. Things closer to the bottom of the pile went into the pile ▬▬.

Appendix G Lesson 90—Fact Game   127

Lesson 90

1	2	3	4	5
6	7	8	9	10
11	12	13	14	15
16	17	18	19	20

The fact game items appear on blackline masters (Appendix G near the back of this guide). Make one copy of the game for each group. Give each group two dice or number cubes.

The answers for the fact games appear at the back of the textbook.

Here are the procedures for playing:

- The monitor is the only person in a group who is permitted to look at the answer page.

- The other players take turns. A player rolls the cubes, adds the numbers showing, reads the item that has the same number, and tells the answer.

- If the player answers correctly, the monitor makes one tally mark in the box at the top of the player's question sheet. Or the monitor says, "Correct," and the player then makes one tally mark.

- The cubes go to the next player (the player to the left), and that player takes a turn.

Here are procedures for setting up the groups:

- If possible, provide a table for each group of players. There should be no obstructions that would prohibit the monitor from observing the players. Players should not be seated directly next to the monitor (where they could read the answers in the monitor's book).

- Each player's scorecard sheet should be on the table, ready for the game.

- If the monitor is to tally each player's correct answers, the monitor should have a pencil. If the monitor is to direct the players to make the tally marks, each player should have a pencil. **Note:** It is important that their scorecards are visible so the monitor can see whether the players are tallying correctly.

Observing the Fact Games

Follow these guidelines when you observe the games.

Reinforce a fast pace. Praise players who have the number cubes ready to roll, find the item quickly, read it correctly, and answer correctly. Remind the players that the faster they play, the more points they can earn. A fast pace also ensures that the players will be less likely to argue with the monitor.

Make comments about each group's progress: Look at how well you're doing. You've already played three rounds. Comments of this type are important because they let the students know that they are part of a group that is working together.

Do not permit the games to drag. If the groups are going slowly, tell the monitor, Come on, let's get this game moving. Nobody's going to earn very many points if they are this slow. A more positive, effective technique is to comment on games that are moving quickly: Wow, this group is really moving. Every player has had five turns already.

Make sure that players are following the rules. After the players have played the game for a few minutes, they may remember what item 5 is or what item 3 is. Therefore, they may attempt to answer the item without first reading the item aloud. For example, they'll say, "Number 3. San Francisco," rather than reading the item, "What place does the letter E show?" Stop players who do not read the item aloud, and remind them of the rule: You must *read* the item aloud and *then* answer it. This stipulation is very important. Many items are included in the game because they are difficult for the students. The difficulty will be reduced greatly if a strong association between the item and the answer is established. This association is ensured, however, only if the students read the item aloud before answering it. Although the students may read it accurately to themselves, the other students in the group will not receive the benefit of hearing the item *and* the answer.

Make sure monitors award points only when the answers are correct. For nearly all items, the correct response is phrased in a very specific way, which is indicated in the answer key.

Unless the player's response is the same as that in the key, the response is incorrect. (There are a few items in later games that permit players to express an idea. For those items, the monitor must use some judgment. For most items, however, very little judgment is required.)

If an answer is not correct, the monitor is to read the correct answer aloud. Students are not permitted to argue with the monitor. If they argue, they lose a turn. The monitors are to raise their hand to signal a problem or a question they can't answer.

Stop the game after it has been played for 10 minutes. When only three minutes of playing time remain, tell the groups: Only 3 minutes more. When the time limit is up, tell the groups to stop: If a player has started a turn, finish that turn. Then the game is over.

Tell each group of players how well they did. Announce which groups played the game smoothly. Tell all students who have more than 10 points to stand up. Congratulate them.

In-Program Tests

Test lessons occur every ten lessons, beginning with lesson 10. Each test consists primarily of content introduced and practiced in the preceding nine lessons. The tests also assess skill items and the vocabulary sentences that students have practiced.

In every test lesson students also do an individual reading checkout. Starting with lesson 30, students play a fact game before taking the test.

Test lessons that have both a written test and individual reading checkout provide you with detailed performance information about individuals and about the group. The test shows you how well individuals and the group comprehend the content that was presented in the different selections, and also shows how well students perform on the skills and vocabulary being taught. The individual reading checkouts give information about how accurately and fluently students read. This package of information permits you to identify specific problems that individual students have, identify problems that are common to more than one student, and provide timely remedies.

Administering the Tests

1. Make sure that students have all materials they need: lined paper, textbook, and pencil.

2. Seat students so they cannot see the work of other students.

3. Direct students to complete the test and turn it in.

4. Score and grade the tests, and perform any necessary remedies before presenting the next lesson.

Scoring the Tests

There are different formats for marking the test, one of which is to perform a workcheck, during which students use a **marking pencil** to indicate which items are wrong (with an **X**). A variation is a workcheck in which students exchange tests and mark each others' tests. A third (and preferable) alternative is for you to score each test.

Even if you do not score each test, you should go over every test and make sure that the marking is accurate. After checking each student's test, write the total number of errors at the top of the test.

Recording Test Performance

You should record each student's performance in two places—on the Group Summary Chart (Appendix H) and on the Test Summary Sheet (Appendix I). A copy of the Test Summary Sheet for tests 1–8 appears below.

You record each student's performance by circling the number of each item the student missed. If the student missed items 3 and 18, you circle the numbers 3 and 18 for that student. The passing criterion for each test is shown at the bottom of the column for each test. Note that the criteria are not the same for different tests. (The criterion for test 2 is 20 correct out of 22, but the criterion for test 5 is 30 correct out of 33.) If the student fails the test, write **F** over the box with item numbers, or circle the box. Either system gives you a quick visual summary of the students who passed versus those who had trouble. In the Test 5 sample on page 70, Denise Barton has a failing score (28 correct out of 33 with passing criterion of 30/33) and so her box has been circled.

Test Summary Sheet

Name	Test 1	Test 2	Test 3	Test 4	Test 5	Test 6	Test 7	Test 8
	1 2 3 4 5 6 / 7 8 9 10 11 12 / 13 14 15 16 17 18 / 19 20 21 22 23 24	1 2 3 4 5 6 / 7 8 9 10 11 12 / 13 14 15 16 17 18 / 19 20 21 22	1 2 3 4 5 6 / 7 8 9 10 11 12 / 13 14 15 16 17 18 / 19 20 21 22 23 24 / 25	1 2 3 4 5 6 / 7 8 9 10 11 12 / 13 14 15 16 17 18 / 19 20 21 22 23 24 / 25 26	1 2 3 4 5 6 / 7 8 9 10 11 12 / 13 14 15 16 17 18 / 19 20 21 22 23 24 / 25 26 27 28 29 30 / 31 32 33	1 2 3 4 5 6 / 7 8 9 10 11 12 / 13 14 15 16 17 18 / 19 20 21 22 23 24 / 25 26 27 28 29 30 / 31 32	1 2 3 4 5 6 / 7 8 9 10 11 12 / 13 14 15 16 17 18 / 19 20 21 22 23 24 / 25 26 27 28 29 30 / 31 32 33 34 35 36	1 2 3 4 5 6 / 7 8 9 10 11 12 / 13 14 15 16 17 18 / 19 20 21 22 23 24 / 25 26 27 28 29
	1 2 3 4 5 6 / 7 8 9 10 11 12 / 13 14 15 16 17 18 / 19 20 21 22 23 24	1 2 3 4 5 6 / 7 8 9 10 11 12 / 13 14 15 16 17 18 / 19 20 21 22	1 2 3 4 5 6 / 7 8 9 10 11 12 / 13 14 15 16 17 18 / 19 20 21 22 23 24 / 25	1 2 3 4 5 6 / 7 8 9 10 11 12 / 13 14 15 16 17 18 / 19 20 21 22 23 24 / 25 26	1 2 3 4 5 6 / 7 8 9 10 11 12 / 13 14 15 16 17 18 / 19 20 21 22 23 24 / 25 26 27 28 29 30 / 31 32 33	1 2 3 4 5 6 / 7 8 9 10 11 12 / 13 14 15 16 17 18 / 19 20 21 22 23 24 / 25 26 27 28 29 30 / 31 32	1 2 3 4 5 6 / 7 8 9 10 11 12 / 13 14 15 16 17 18 / 19 20 21 22 23 24 / 25 26 27 28 29 30 / 31 32 33 34 35 36	1 2 3 4 5 6 / 7 8 9 10 11 12 / 13 14 15 16 17 18 / 19 20 21 22 23 24 / 25 26 27 28 29
	1 2 3 4 5 6 / 7 8 9 10 11 12 / 13 14 15 16 17 18 / 19 20 21 22 23 24	1 2 3 4 5 6 / 7 8 9 10 11 12 / 13 14 15 16 17 18 / 19 20 21 22	1 2 3 4 5 6 / 7 8 9 10 11 12 / 13 14 15 16 17 18 / 19 20 21 22 23 24 / 25	1 2 3 4 5 6 / 7 8 9 10 11 12 / 13 14 15 16 17 18 / 19 20 21 22 23 24 / 25 26	1 2 3 4 5 6 / 7 8 9 10 11 12 / 13 14 15 16 17 18 / 19 20 21 22 23 24 / 25 26 27 28 29 30 / 31 32 33	1 2 3 4 5 6 / 7 8 9 10 11 12 / 13 14 15 16 17 18 / 19 20 21 22 23 24 / 25 26 27 28 29 30 / 31 32	1 2 3 4 5 6 / 7 8 9 10 11 12 / 13 14 15 16 17 18 / 19 20 21 22 23 24 / 25 26 27 28 29 30 / 31 32 33 34 35 36	1 2 3 4 5 6 / 7 8 9 10 11 12 / 13 14 15 16 17 18 / 19 20 21 22 23 24 / 25 26 27 28 29
	1 2 3 4 5 6 / 7 8 9 10 11 12 / 13 14 15 16 17 18 / 19 20 21 22 23 24	1 2 3 4 5 6 / 7 8 9 10 11 12 / 13 14 15 16 17 18 / 19 20 21 22	1 2 3 4 5 6 / 7 8 9 10 11 12 / 13 14 15 16 17 18 / 19 20 21 22 23 24 / 25	1 2 3 4 5 6 / 7 8 9 10 11 12 / 13 14 15 16 17 18 / 19 20 21 22 23 24 / 25 26	1 2 3 4 5 6 / 7 8 9 10 11 12 / 13 14 15 16 17 18 / 19 20 21 22 23 24 / 25 26 27 28 29 30 / 31 32 33	1 2 3 4 5 6 / 7 8 9 10 11 12 / 13 14 15 16 17 18 / 19 20 21 22 23 24 / 25 26 27 28 29 30 / 31 32	1 2 3 4 5 6 / 7 8 9 10 11 12 / 13 14 15 16 17 18 / 19 20 21 22 23 24 / 25 26 27 28 29 30 / 31 32 33 34 35 36	1 2 3 4 5 6 / 7 8 9 10 11 12 / 13 14 15 16 17 18 / 19 20 21 22 23 24 / 25 26 27 28 29
	1 2 3 4 5 6 / 7 8 9 10 11 12 / 13 14 15 16 17 18 / 19 20 21 22 23 24	1 2 3 4 5 6 / 7 8 9 10 11 12 / 13 14 15 16 17 18 / 19 20 21 22	1 2 3 4 5 6 / 7 8 9 10 11 12 / 13 14 15 16 17 18 / 19 20 21 22 23 24 / 25	1 2 3 4 5 6 / 7 8 9 10 11 12 / 13 14 15 16 17 18 / 19 20 21 22 23 24 / 25 26	1 2 3 4 5 6 / 7 8 9 10 11 12 / 13 14 15 16 17 18 / 19 20 21 22 23 24 / 25 26 27 28 29 30 / 31 32 33	1 2 3 4 5 6 / 7 8 9 10 11 12 / 13 14 15 16 17 18 / 19 20 21 22 23 24 / 25 26 27 28 29 30 / 31 32	1 2 3 4 5 6 / 7 8 9 10 11 12 / 13 14 15 16 17 18 / 19 20 21 22 23 24 / 25 26 27 28 29 30 / 31 32 33 34 35 36	1 2 3 4 5 6 / 7 8 9 10 11 12 / 13 14 15 16 17 18 / 19 20 21 22 23 24 / 25 26 27 28 29
	1 2 3 4 5 6 / 7 8 9 10 11 12 / 13 14 15 16 17 18 / 19 20 21 22 23 24	1 2 3 4 5 6 / 7 8 9 10 11 12 / 13 14 15 16 17 18 / 19 20 21 22	1 2 3 4 5 6 / 7 8 9 10 11 12 / 13 14 15 16 17 18 / 19 20 21 22 23 24 / 25	1 2 3 4 5 6 / 7 8 9 10 11 12 / 13 14 15 16 17 18 / 19 20 21 22 23 24 / 25 26	1 2 3 4 5 6 / 7 8 9 10 11 12 / 13 14 15 16 17 18 / 19 20 21 22 23 24 / 25 26 27 28 29 30 / 31 32 33	1 2 3 4 5 6 / 7 8 9 10 11 12 / 13 14 15 16 17 18 / 19 20 21 22 23 24 / 25 26 27 28 29 30 / 31 32	1 2 3 4 5 6 / 7 8 9 10 11 12 / 13 14 15 16 17 18 / 19 20 21 22 23 24 / 25 26 27 28 29 30 / 31 32 33 34 35 36	1 2 3 4 5 6 / 7 8 9 10 11 12 / 13 14 15 16 17 18 / 19 20 21 22 23 24 / 25 26 27 28 29
	1 2 3 4 5 6 / 7 8 9 10 11 12 / 13 14 15 16 17 18 / 19 20 21 22 23 24	1 2 3 4 5 6 / 7 8 9 10 11 12 / 13 14 15 16 17 18 / 19 20 21 22	1 2 3 4 5 6 / 7 8 9 10 11 12 / 13 14 15 16 17 18 / 19 20 21 22 23 24 / 25	1 2 3 4 5 6 / 7 8 9 10 11 12 / 13 14 15 16 17 18 / 19 20 21 22 23 24 / 25 26	1 2 3 4 5 6 / 7 8 9 10 11 12 / 13 14 15 16 17 18 / 19 20 21 22 23 24 / 25 26 27 28 29 30 / 31 32 33	1 2 3 4 5 6 / 7 8 9 10 11 12 / 13 14 15 16 17 18 / 19 20 21 22 23 24 / 25 26 27 28 29 30 / 31 32	1 2 3 4 5 6 / 7 8 9 10 11 12 / 13 14 15 16 17 18 / 19 20 21 22 23 24 / 25 26 27 28 29 30 / 31 32 33 34 35 36	1 2 3 4 5 6 / 7 8 9 10 11 12 / 13 14 15 16 17 18 / 19 20 21 22 23 24 / 25 26 27 28 29
	1 2 3 4 5 6 / 7 8 9 10 11 12 / 13 14 15 16 17 18 / 19 20 21 22 23 24	1 2 3 4 5 6 / 7 8 9 10 11 12 / 13 14 15 16 17 18 / 19 20 21 22	1 2 3 4 5 6 / 7 8 9 10 11 12 / 13 14 15 16 17 18 / 19 20 21 22 23 24 / 25	1 2 3 4 5 6 / 7 8 9 10 11 12 / 13 14 15 16 17 18 / 19 20 21 22 23 24 / 25 26	1 2 3 4 5 6 / 7 8 9 10 11 12 / 13 14 15 16 17 18 / 19 20 21 22 23 24 / 25 26 27 28 29 30 / 31 32 33	1 2 3 4 5 6 / 7 8 9 10 11 12 / 13 14 15 16 17 18 / 19 20 21 22 23 24 / 25 26 27 28 29 30 / 31 32	1 2 3 4 5 6 / 7 8 9 10 11 12 / 13 14 15 16 17 18 / 19 20 21 22 23 24 / 25 26 27 28 29 30 / 31 32 33 34 35 36	1 2 3 4 5 6 / 7 8 9 10 11 12 / 13 14 15 16 17 18 / 19 20 21 22 23 24 / 25 26 27 28 29
Passing Criterion	22/24	20/22	22/25	23/26	30/33	29/32	32/36	26/29

Teacher __Ms. Turner__   Group __2__

Name	Lessons 41 IW	42 IW	43 IW	44 IW	CO 45 CO	45 IW	46 IW	47 IW	48 IW	49 IW	CO/Test 5 CO	Test
Main Story Errors	7	8	8	8	(9)	11	7	5	9			
Luis Cepeda	2	1	2	1	P / 0	2	1	0	1	3	P / 0	2
Yoko Higashi	(4)	3	2	2	P / 0	2	3	1	2	2	P / 1	2
Anita Diaz	1	1	1	0	P / 0	2	1	1	0	2	P / 0	0
Denise Barton	1	2	0	1	(F) / 1	1	0	1	0	2	P / 2	(5)
Zachary Gray	1	0	0	1	P / 0	1	2	1	1	1	P / 0	0
Eric Adler	2	1	1	0	P / 1	1	0	1	0	2	P / 1	2

You should also record each student's test performance on the Group Summary Chart. In the **Test** column, write the number of errors each student made on the test. Circle any number that exceeds the passing criterion for the test.

The sample Group Summary Chart above has been filled out for lessons 41 through 50 (test 5). The shaded column shows the part of the chart used for recording test 5 performance. (Denise Barton missed 5 out of 33 items. Her failing score has been circled.)

Test Remedies

Reproducible blackline masters of the Test Summary Sheets appear in Appendix I. The Test Summary Sheets provide an item-by-item analysis of the errors each student made. This information implies the kind of remedies that should be provided (ideally before you present the next lesson). A sample Test Summary for test 5 has been filled out and appears on the next page.

Total Errors

The total errors a student made tells you whether the student is progressing adequately. Students who exceed the specified number of errors are not performing at a level required to thoroughly comprehend the material they read.

Error Patterns

The basic patterns that you should look for when summarizing the data are: (a) a student (or groups of students) who fails the passing criterion on two or more consecutive tests; (b) the same item (or group of related items) being missed by more than 1/4 of the students.

Test Summary Sheet

Name _____ Test 5

Name	Test 5
Luis Cepeda	1 2 ③ 4 5 6 / 7 8 ⑨ 10 11 12 / ⒔ 14 15 16 17 18 / ⑲ 20 21 22 23 24 / 25 26 27 28 29 30 / 31 32 33
Yoko Higashi	1 2 3 4 5 6 / 7 8 9 10 11 12 / ⒔ 14 15 16 17 18 / ⑲ 20 21 22 23 24 / 25 26 ㉗ 28 29 30 / 31 32 33
Anita Diaz	1 2 3 4 5 6 / 7 8 9 10 11 12 / 13 14 15 16 17 18 / 19 20 21 22 23 24 / 25 26 27 28 29 30 / 31 32 33
Denise Barton	1 2 ③ 4 5 ⑥ / 7 8 ⑨ 10 11 ⑫ / 13 14 15 ⑯ 17 18 / ⑲ 20 21 22 23 24 / ㉕ 26 ㉗ 28 29 30 / 31 32 ㉝
Zachary Gray	1 2 3 4 5 6 / 7 8 9 10 11 12 / 13 14 15 16 17 18 / 19 20 21 22 23 24 / 25 26 27 28 29 30 / 31 32 33
Eric Adler	1 2 ③ 4 5 6 / 7 8 ⑨ 10 11 12 / 13 ⒕ 15 16 17 18 / 19 ⑳ 21 22 23 24 / 25 26 27 28 29 30 / 31 32 33
	1 2 3 4 5 6 / 7 8 9 10 11 12 / 13 14 15 16 17 18 / 19 20 21 22 23 24 / 25 26 27 28 29 30 / 31 32 33
	1 2 3 4 5 6 / 7 8 9 10 11 12 / 13 14 15 16 17 18 / 19 20 21 22 23 24 / 25 26 27 28 29 30 / 31 32 33
Passing Criterion	30/33

Students Who Fail Consecutive Tests

Any student who fails consecutive tests is probably misplaced in the program. If more than one or two students exhibit this pattern, there are probably problems with the way the material is being presented, reviewed, and firmed. The first step in remediation would be to make sure that the students are trying. The simplest way is to provide them with some sort of reward or positive response for meeting the criterion on tests. For example, make a chart that shows the number of students who pass each test. Have a party or some special award for students who pass two or more consecutive tests. Also make sure that you have a solid workcheck and that students are doing the fact games.

In some cases, you will have students who do not really belong in the program—based on their reading performance—and there is no possibility of putting them in another group. Although you teach carefully, these students still do not perform at criterion. The best practice in this case is to do what you can in firming these students and providing additional practice **outside the regular reading periods.** But when you are teaching the reading group, do not gear the rate of the presentation to these students. Rather, gear it to the students who are appropriately placed in the program. If you gear the presentation to the students who are misplaced, you will go far too slowly for the others, and the presentation will be boring.

Students Who Fail the Same Items

If 1/4 or more of the students fail the same item or group of related items, those items require more practice and review. Here are the remediation steps.

1. Identify the common items that are missed, and create a fact review that involves these items.

A Test Firming Table for each test appears in the teacher presentation book, at the end of the test lesson. You may use this table to help you construct fact reviews (or to firm specific concepts). The table lists the test items and indicates the first lesson in which that item appeared. Here is the table for test 5.

Test 5 Firming Table					
Test Item	Introduced in lesson	Test Item	Introduced in lesson	Test Item	Introduced in lesson
1	41	12	46	23	48
2	41	13	46	24	48
3	41	14	49	25	48
4	42	15	49	26	46
5	42	16	49	27	41
6	42	17	49	28	45
7	44	18	49	29	37
8	44	19	41	30	37
9	44	20	44	31	45
10	46	21	44	32	41
11	46	22	44	33	41

According to the Test 5 summary sample on page 69, 1/4 of the students missed items 9 and 19.

9. When a plane flies from New York City to San Francisco, is it flying in the **same direction** or the **opposite direction** as the wind?

19. What's the boiling temperature of water?
   • 212 miles   • 112 degrees   • 212 degree

By checking the Test 5 Firming Table, we see that item 9 was introduced in lesson 44, and item 19 in lesson 41.

Now create a fact review that involves these items. (See page 58 and **Note** below.)

2. Present the fact review as part of the test remedy and then as part of subsequent lessons.

3. Present the items until the students are quite firm—virtually flawless.

4. If the number of students who had difficulties is large, present the review to the entire reading group.

Note: If students miss skill items or vocabulary items, you can follow a similar procedure in making up a fact review. For example, if students have trouble identifying what somebody said in sentences, you could say different sentences, and direct students to say what the person said. For example:

"My, my," she said. "What a nice day." Tell me everything the girl said.

If students have trouble with deductions, present the first part of different deductions and direct students to say the conclusion. For example:

Fish live in water. A mackerel is a fish. So . . .

Sometimes, the trend is predictable. If there has been a substitute for several lessons before the test, the students probably will perform more poorly than they would if you had been working with them. The remedy is not only to go over the information that relates to the items the students tended to miss, but also to go over information that is closely related. For example, if students tend to miss three items about the nervous system, they would probably miss other items about the nervous system that were not on the test. Go over the independent work for the lessons that introduce the nervous system, and identify all key items. (The Test Firming Table in the teacher presentation book indicates the key lessons where items are introduced.) Present those items in a fact-review format. (This review is probably best presented to the entire reading group, not to only those students who had serious problems.)

Use a variation of the same procedure if the pattern occurs on material that you had presented. Sometimes students get overloaded with information. First see if the items they miss are related. If they are, refer to the independent-work items, and identify all the major facts that are related to the items the students missed. Present those facts in a fact-review format.

Retesting Students

After you have provided remedies, a general rule is to **retest students who failed.**

Do not retest the students after you simply mark answers on their test. Provide a remedy first. Before retesting make sure that they can respond correctly to the various items they missed. One purpose of the retest is to document that the remedy has worked. Another is to show the students that they can perform well on the tests and to provide them with the practice they need to achieve mastery.

Grades

The purpose of letter or number grades is to show the progress and skill level of the students. If students pass the tests consistently, and generally do not make more than three errors on their independent work, they deserve an A. The number grade would be over 90.

A student should be able to fail one or two tests and still earn an A. The reason is that some tests present difficult items.

The simplest grading system is to use the letter grades of A and F or U (for unsatisfactory). If students tend to meet criterion on independent work and tests, they receive an A. Otherwise, they receive a letter that suggests they are not performing adequately. Awarding Bs and Cs is difficult because the passing criteria for tests and independent work are quite high (sometimes above 90%). Students who average much below 90% are not performing adequately. If students do not meet the passing criteria for worksheets and tests, their percentage of correct responses may still be in the 80% range, but they are not performing at the level of mastery that is required by the program.

Writing and Spelling Lessons

Specifications for 131 writing-spelling lessons appear in the Writing and Spelling Guide. Writing-spelling lessons appear as part of all lessons except test lessons.

The writing-spelling lessons are not to be presented during the reading period. Rather, a daily 10-minute writing-spelling period should occur at some other time of the day (except test-lesson days).

Writing

The writing activities consist of two types: sentence copying and main-idea sentences. Sentence copying runs from lesson 11 through lesson 75. Main idea items start in lesson 76 and are presented in every lesson through the end of the program.

Sentence Copying

The main purpose of these activities is to develop fluency in writing and familiarity with conventions, such as the use of question marks, quote marks, apostrophes, periods, and capital letters. Fluency in writing and familiarity with conventions are very important. When students who are not fluent try to write coherent sentences, they often forget what they are trying to write and produce very stilted work. Students who are fluent are in a much better position to express their thoughts.

Here are some examples of the sentences introduced in *Reading Mastery Plus* Level 3:

What direction is the wind?
(Lesson 21)

Are you glad that you're small?
(Lesson 27)

When she grew, she was happy.
(Lesson 36)

Troy is now part of Turkey.
(Lesson 65)

They said, "Let's have a party."
(Lesson 67)

For each copying activity, you write the sentence on the board and direct the students to copy the sentence more than one time. Until lesson 34, they copy the sentence two more times. Beginning with lesson 34, they copy the sentence as many times as they can in three minutes. Here's the exercise from lesson 36.

SENTENCE COPYING

a. (Write on the board:)

> **When she grew, she was happy.**

b. You're going to write this sentence.
   - (Call on a student to read the sentence.)
c. Everybody, turn your paper over. ✔
   - Copy the sentence on the top line. Do it quickly.
   (Observe students and give feedback.)
d. Pencils down. You're going to copy the sentence as many times as you can in three minutes. Get ready. Go. **(Time the students. At the end of three minutes, say:)** Stop. Pencils down.
   - (Call on individual students.) How many times did you copy the sentence?

Writing Main Idea Sentences

Main idea sentences are introduced in lesson 76. During the pre-writing activities, you model several sentences, then call on individual students to generate other sentences. The writing assignment for the students is to write a main-idea sentence. Initially, they may write one of the sentences that has been presented or a new one.

These early sentences are about characters from the Bertha stories. The students are to start the sentence with the character's name and then tell about an "important" thing the character did.

Here's the exercise from lesson 76.

WRITING

a. (Write on the board:)

> **Bertha**
> **Maria**

- You're going to write two sentences that tell one of the important things each of these characters did in today's story.
b. Here's an important thing that Bertha did. Listen: Bertha hid in the back of the van. Everybody, say that sentence. Get ready. (Signal.) *Bertha hid in the back of the van.*
   - Here's an important thing that **Maria** did: Maria held the water near the van. Everybody, say that sentence. Get ready. (Signal.) *Maria held the water near the van.*
   - Who can make up another sentence that tells another important thing that **Bertha** did? (Call on individual students. Direct the group to repeat acceptable sentences. Ideas: *Bertha fainted; Bertha got very hot and dizzy.*)
c. You're going to write a sentence about Bertha on your lined paper. Start the sentence with the name **Bertha.** Remember the capital **B.** Then write something important that she did. At the end of your sentence make a period. If you don't know how to spell a word, write it the way it sounds. Raise your hand when you're finished.
   (Observe students and give feedback.)
d. (Call on individual students to write their sentences on the board. Praise good sentences.)
e. Now you're going to write a sentence about Maria. Start with the name **Maria.** Remember the capital **M.** Then write something important that she did. At the end of your sentence make a period. If you don't know how to spell a word, write it the way it sounds. Raise your hand when you're finished.
   (Observe students and give feedback.)
f. (Call on individual students to write their sentences on the board. Praise good sentences.)

In lesson 79, the procedure is greatly faded. For these exercises, you do not model any sentences, but you call on students to make up sentences. (They are to follow the same procedure specified for the earlier exercises. They start with the name of the character and then tell about something important that character did.) Here's the exercise from lesson 79.

WRITING

a. You're going to write one sentence that tells an important thing a character did in today's story.
b. Name a character. (Call on a student.)
 • Raise your hand if you can make up a sentence that starts with that character's name and tells an important thing the character did. (Direct the group to repeat acceptable sentences.)
c. Everybody, write a sentence about a character in today's story. Remember, the name is capitalized wherever it appears in the sentence. Raise your hand when you're finished.
 (Observe students and give feedback.)
d. (Call on individual students to write their sentences on the board. Praise good sentences.)

If you feel that students do not need the structure indicated in the exercise, drop step b of the exercise. Use the same criterion established for oral sentences in step b to evaluate the students' written work. The sentence is to start with the character's name and is to tell about something important—not trivial. There should be a period at the end of the sentence. Familiar spelling words should be spelled correctly.

Spelling

The spelling component of *Reading Mastery Plus* Level 3 is to be presented at a time other than the period for reading. Each spelling lesson takes about five minutes. It begins with lesson 1 of the reading program and is a part of every lesson except test lessons through the end of the program. (The first spelling lesson is lesson 1, and it is to be presented on the same day Reading lesson 1 is presented.)

Scope

The spelling component introduces words with multiple-consonant beginnings and endings (<u>dr</u>ip, <u>fl</u>ame, ca<u>mp</u>, ba<u>nd</u>), different letter combinations (th, sh, ch, ea, ou, ar, al, or, ol, oi, oy, aw, oo), rules for adding endings to words, and the procedures for writing compound words. Write the first part; then, without leaving a space, write the second part. The main objective of the spelling lesson is to reinforce what students learn about reading. As part of the spelling lesson, students learn to identify vowels and consonants, and later use these skills to figure out the spelling of different words with endings. A Scope and Sequence chart for the Writing and Spelling components appears in the *Writing and Spelling Guide.*

Sequence

The general rule for the first 25 spelling lessons is that if students say the sounds for any word they are to spell, they will know how to spell the word. There is no ambiguity; these words are spelled the way they sound. The word "meet" could be spelled different ways with "legitimate" spellings for the long-**E** sound **(mete, meet, meat),** therefore, it does not appear in the first 25 spelling lessons. The word **met,** however, has one possible spelling. By saying the three sounds in **met** and by writing the only letter known to the student for each sound, the student will spell the word correctly.

The general sequencing procedure for the program is that a new skill or word type is introduced and practiced for a few lessons. Then the new skill or type is consolidated (the new type and the earlier-taught word types appearing in the same practice lists). The lists assure that students learn to distinguish among all the various types that have been taught. For instance, after students have learned beginnings and endings spelled with **sh, th, ch,** they learn words that have the combination **al (all)** or **ar (are).** After practicing **ar** and **al** words exclusively for several lessons, students next do a series of consolidation exercises that present a mix of **ar** words and all the other types that have been practiced earlier (including words like **charm**).

Through lesson 4, students continue to practice words with the short vowel sounds, with some emphasis on multiple-consonant beginnings and endings (**mp, nt, pl, br,** etc.).

The combinations that students have learned in reading appear in the spelling exercises, starting with lesson 5. New combinations are introduced every few lessons (on the average) throughout the program. The combinations include **ea, oo, aw, oy, oi, ou.** For some combina-

tions, the program provides general rules. For instance, if a word ends with the sound "oy" it is spelled **O-Y.** If the sound "oy" occurs in the middle of the word, it is spelled **O-I.** Similarly, the long-**A** sound at the end of a word is spelled **A-Y.** The same sound in the middle of the word can be spelled different ways—**A-I, A** with a final **E,** or just **A.**

Starting with lesson 6, students identify vowels. Beginning with lesson 11, students also identify consonants. Here's part of the exercise from lesson 6.

SPELLING

a. (Write on the board:)

a	e	i	o	u	y

- For some of the work you'll do in reading and spelling, you have to know some rules about vowels and consonants.
- Here's one rule: The vowel letters are **A, E, I, O, U,** and sometimes **Y.** Listen again: **A, E, I, O, U,** and sometimes **Y.**
- Name the vowel letters. Get ready. (Signal.) *A, E, I, O, U, and sometimes Y.*
- (Repeat until firm.)
- All the other letters are consonants. What do we call the other letters? (Signal.) *Consonants.*
- Say the vowel letters again. Get ready. (Signal.) *A, E, I, O, U, and sometimes Y.*

b. I'll say some letters. You tell me if they are **vowels** or **consonants.**
- Listen: **B.** Tell me. Get ready. (Signal.) *Consonant.*
- **E.** Tell me. Get ready. (Signal.) *Vowel.*
- **O.** Tell me. Get ready. (Signal.) *Vowel.*
- **L.** Tell me. Get ready. (Signal.) *Consonant.*
- **R.** Tell me. Get ready. (Signal.) *Consonant.*
- **I.** Tell me. Get ready. (Signal.) *Vowel.*

c. (Write on the board:)

1. clean	4. rub
2. fine	5. lock
3. flame	

- Each word has one or more vowel letters. Copy the words. Be sure to spell them correctly. Raise your hand when you're finished.
  (Observe students and give feedback.)
d. Underline every vowel letter in the words you copied. Raise your hand when you're finished.
  (Observe students and give feedback.)
e. Check your work. Make an **X** next to any word you got wrong.
f. Word 1 is **clean.** What are the vowel letters? (Signal.) *E and A.*
- Word 2 is **fine.** What are the vowel letters? (Signal.) *I and E.*
- Word 3 is **flame.** What are the vowel letters? (Signal.) *A and E.*
- Word 4 is **rub.** What's the vowel letter? (Signal.) *U.*
- Word 5 is **lock.** What's the vowel letter? (Signal.) *O.*

In lesson 37, students learn that they can add the ending **S** to words without changing the spelling of the word. In lesson 44, students add the endings **ed, ing,** and **er** to words. Note that the last three letters in these words are **not** consonant-vowel-consonant. Therefore, students are not required to change the spelling of these words. Here's the list of words from lesson 44: **salted, farmer, starting, dreamer, planted.** Note that the root words are words that students have practiced earlier.

In lesson 51, students learn the spelling of the endings **est, ful,** and **ly.** They add these endings to words that do not end in consonant-vowel-consonant. Here are the words from lesson 51: **cleanest, handful, coldest, clearly, harmful.**

Finally, in lesson 102, students write words that have the endings **en** or **less.**

A major skill is introduced in lesson 85. Students learn words that have a long-vowel sound and are spelled with a final **E** (**home, safe, shine,** etc.). Students first practice with a small set of these words. Practice is limited to a small set because there is nothing in the pronunciation of these words to suggest how the long-vowel sound is spelled. When you hear the word **rode** in isolation, you don't know if it is spelled **R-O-D-E** or **R-O-A-D.** By practicing a small set of words, students learn, through stipulation, that these words are spelled with a final **E.** The set includes: **take, time, nose, close, kite, shine, safe, game, name, home, make.**

These words are consolidated by being presented in lists that have other words students have learned. For instance, in lesson 92, students spell these words: **found, time, meal, spoon, life.** Note that three of the words (**time, meal, life**) have a letter that says its name. Two of these words (**time, life**) are spelled with a final **E.** The word **meal** does not have a final **E.** Students probably would not write the word as **M-E-L-E** (even if they had not practiced the word before) because nearly all the long-**E**-vowel words they have practiced are spelled with **E-A.**

In lesson 94, students practice adding endings to words that do not end in consonant-vowel-consonant. Students copy words, write **C** or **V** above the last three letters in each word, and write endings for words that do not end in **C-V-C.** Here's the list of words from lesson 94: **hang, sleep, drop, scrub, plant, preach.** They cross out the words that end in **C-V-C** (**drop, scrub**). They write **er** on the other words: **hanger, sleeper, planter, preacher.**

Students practice with similar exercises until lesson 101, when they learn the rule for adding **er, ed,** and **ing** to words that do end in **C-V-C.** The rule: If the word ends in **C-V-C,** double the last letter before writing the ending. Here are the words presented in lesson 101: **slap, brag, greet, fill, fan, bug.** Two of the words **(greet, fill)** do not end in **C-V-C,** so students simply add the ending **E-D** to these words: **greeted, filled.** For the other words, they double the final consonant and then write the ending: **slapped, bragged, fanned, bugged.**

In lesson 106, students learn to process words that end in a final **E.** The words are presented in a list that has other types: **hate, time, bat, plan, shine, trap.** Students first underline the words that end in **C-V-C (bat, plan, trap).** Next, students fix up all the words so they end in **E-D.** For the words that end in **E,** students add only **D.** For the other words, students double the final consonant and add **E-D.**

Students work with similar lists through lesson 114, adding the endings **E-D** and **E-R.** Students then learn the rule for adding **I-N-G** to words that end in **E.** Here are the words students change: **make, sit, greet, hope, hop, like.** For the words that end in **C-V-C,** students double the final consonant and write the ending **I-N-G (sitting, hopping).** The other words do not end in **C-V-C,** so it is not necessary to double the final consonant. For the words that end in a final **E (make, hope, like)** students cross out the final **E** and then write **I-N-G (making, hoping, liking).**

Starting with lesson 135, students write compound words. As part of this work, they learn to spell **some, one, any, every, body,** and **thing.**

The initial compound words students spell include **anyone, however, nobody, everyone,** and **something.**

Starting with lesson 137, students spell other words that are composed of familiar component words, for example **runway, bedroom, outside, football, tonight, snapshot, overtime, whenever, downtown, yourself, another, without.**

For a complete alphabetical listing of all spelling words taught in the program, see Appendix E.

Literature Book Component

Literature Lessons

The literature component of *Reading Mastery Plus* Level 3 consists of a presentation book *Literature Guide*, one "Read-to" book, and copies of the student literature anthology that are used in the literature lessons. The presentation book includes directions for the lessons and blackline masters that are to be reproduced as student material.

Literature Selections

Literature lessons present stories, poems, and a play. The following chart lists the selections and the lessons in which they are to be presented.

Presented with Lesson	Literature Lesson	Title	Author
6	1	Introduction of Literary Elements	
10	2	*Stephanie's Ponytail*	Robert Munsch
20	3	*George at the Zoo*	Sally George
30	4-1	*A House with a Star Inside*	Retold by Melissa Heckler
	4-2	*Remember* (poem)	Pamela Mordecai
40	5	*Pop's Truck*	Honey Anderson and Bill Reinholtd
50	6	*Trixie*	Rick Brownell
60	7	*The Three Wishes*	Told by Margo Zemach
70	8	*Tom's Friend*	Pat Reynolds
80	9-1	*The Case of Natty Nat*	Donald Sobol
	9-2	*Swap* (poem)	Carol Diggory Shields
90	10-1	*The Thirsty Crows*	Faye W. Daggett
	10-2	*Rabbit* (poem)	Pamela Mordecai
100	11	*Moonwalker* (poem)	Carol Diggory Shields
110	12	*See the Rabbits—Part 1*	Harvey Cleaver
115	13	*See the Rabbits—Part 2*	Harvey Cleaver
120	14	*The Proud Crow* (play)	Adapted by Fran Lehr
130	15	*The Fox and the Crow*	Retold by Faye W. Daggett
140	16	*The Magic Teakettle*	Harriet Winfield

Time Requirements

All but two of the literature lessons are scheduled every 10 lessons, starting with lesson 10, and follow each 10-lesson test. The literature lesson does not have to be scheduled on the same day as the test, and it should not be scheduled as part of the regular reading lesson. The literature lessons are a treat. Schedule each activity for 40–80 minutes. The lesson with a "Read-to" selection (lesson 80) may be presented on two separate days.

Materials

In addition to the anthologies and the blackline masters, students need specific materials for the scheduled activities. The teacher presentation for each lesson in the Literature Guide specifies what materials are needed. (The major supplies that students need for these lessons are lined paper, crayons, scissors, tape, and paste.)

Preparation

Before presenting each literature lesson, read the scheduled activity, secure the materials, and copy the blackline masters.

Presenting the Lessons

Each literature lesson is based on a theme from the selection. The following chart lists the lesson themes and gives a brief summary of the primary expansion activities for each lesson.

Themes and Activities

Literature Lesson	Presented with Lesson	Theme	Primary Expansion Activities
2. *Stephanie's Ponytail*	10	Individual tastes vary	Teacher conducts a poll and produces a bar graph showing students' favorite and least favorite hairdos.
3. *George at the Zoo*	20	Bravery; misbehavior	Students arrange animal pictures to show strength hierarchy; students write a behavior-change program for a pet that misbehaves.
4-1. *A House with a Star Inside*	30	Riddles	Students discuss the riddle presented in the story; students solve riddles about foods; students write riddles about foods.
4-2. *Remember*	30	Changes; memories	Students make up additional parts of the poem; students draw pictures for some of the poem descriptions; students research and do a report on the poem's author.
5. *Pop's Truck*	40	Old friends; recycling	Students write about a favorite belonging; teacher produces a chart of students' favorite belongings; students write about how some old objects could be reused for another purpose.
6. *Trixie*	50	Handicaps; individual differences	Students compare the stories *Pop's Truck* and *Trixie*; students discuss and write about how people with handicaps could compensate for their handicaps.

Literature Lesson	Presented with Lesson	Theme	Primary Expansion Activities
7. *The Three Wishes*	60	Comparing others with ourselves; greed	Students discuss and write about a person who thinks the student's home is like a palace; students write three wishes; teacher produces a bar graph of students' wishes.
8. *Tom's Friend*	70	Freedom	Students discuss the main character's ability to assume another perspective; students write a report that requires them to assume another perspective; students create a display on "Thinking like someone else."
9-1. (Read to) *The Case of Natty Nat*	80*	Self-contradiction	Students rewrite the end of the story.
9-2. *Swap*	80	Changes don't always lead to change.	None
10-1. *The Thirsty Crows*	90	Persistence	Students write and illustrate their own stories of persistence.
10-2. *Rabbit*	90	Pets	Students research how to care for a pet rabbit.
11. *Moonwalker*	100	Imagination	Students draw a picture or write a story about something they imagine doing, but have never done.
12. *See the Rabbits Part 1*	110	Misunderstanding	Using a map, students figure out where the story characters may be traveling to.
13. *See the Rabbits Part 2*	115	Misunderstanding	Students write a story based on misunderstanding what someone said.
14. *The Proud Crow*	120	Vanity	Students make or gather props, stage settings and costumes, and then put on a reading version of the play.
15. *The Fox and the Crow*	130	Vanity	Students compare and contrast *The Proud Crow* and *The Fox and the Crow*.
16. *The Magic Teakettle*	140	Good fortune; appearances; keeping promises	Students create props, develop narration, and put on a play based on the story.

*Note that selection 9-1 is a "Read to" selection that does not appear in the student literature anthology. It may be presented separately at a later time.

Language Arts Guide

Directions and blackline masters for 90 lessons appear in the Language Arts Guide. These lessons occur daily beginning with lesson 51.

The lessons in the Language Arts Guide are not to be presented during the reading period. Instead, a daily 10 to 15 minute period should occur at another time of the day.

Content

The Language Arts Guide develops three major skill areas: book parts, alphabetizing, and affixes. The guide also presents more than 35 exercises that deal with specific writing, grammar, and comprehension skills.

The scope-and-sequence chart below shows the four main tracks that the guide develops. Note that most lessons present two exercises.

Book Parts

The track starts on lesson 51 and continues through lesson 140. The lessons teach students about the following parts of books: table of contents, index, and glossary.

During the early lessons, students learn about the table of contents—what kind of

	51	52	53	54	55	56	57	58	59	60	61	62
Book Parts					table of contents							
Alphabetizing											1st letter	
Writing, Grammar, and Comprehension			subject-verb agreement									

	81	82	83	84	85	86	87	88	89	90	91	92
Alphabetizing	1st 2 letters											
Affixes			dis		re		un		less		ful	ness
Writing, Grammar, and Comprehension		writing										

	111	112	113	114	115	116	117	118	119	120	121	122
Book Parts									index			
Alphabetizing				dictionary								
Writing, Grammar, and Comprehension			idioms, similes, synonyms, opposites									

information the table gives and how to use the table to find specific selections in the book. Later in the program, beginning on lesson 119, students learn to use the index, which appears in the back of textbook C.

Starting on lesson 128, after students have learned about the table of contents, the index and the glossary, they do items that require them to indicate the book part they would use to find the answer to specific items, such as:

- You want to find out what the word **rescue** means.

- You want to find out the first page number for the topic *time lines.*

- You want to find out the page number for the first selection in lesson 125.

Alphabetizing

The track starts on lesson 61 and continues through lesson 118. For the first exercises students alphabetize word lists that require reference to only the first letter. Beginning in lesson 67, they work with word lists that require attending to the first two letters of each word. Students learn about guide words starting in lesson 100 and apply alphabetizing skills to the guide words of the glossary. Finally, starting in lesson 108, students apply their alphabetizing skills to the dictionary.

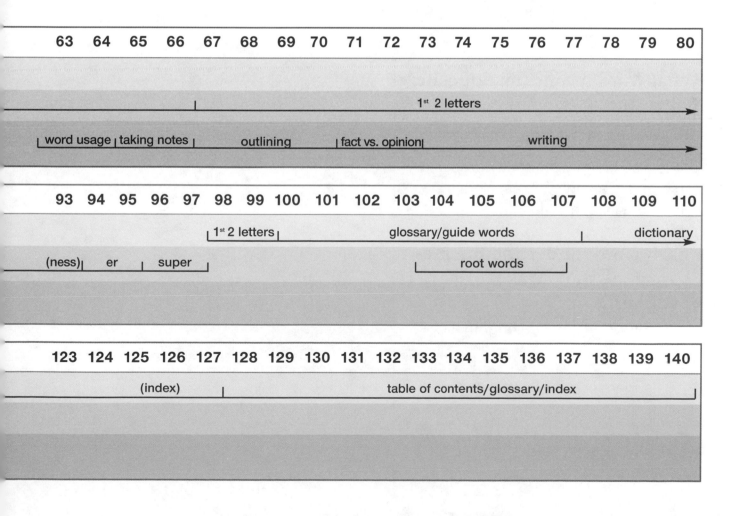

Affixes

This track begins on lesson 83 and continues through lesson 107. The affixes that students study are those that have stable meanings and that are fairly common: **dis, re, un, less, ful, ness, er,** and **super.** Students learn to classify these parts as prefixes or suffixes. They also learn about common root words and how affixes are combined with root words to form new words with predictable meanings. Here are some of the items that students work:

Write the word for each description.

1. What word means **to tell again?**

   _____

2. What word means **not able?**

   _____

   .
   .
   .

5. What word means **the opposite of continue?**

   _____

Students also identify the root words and possible prefixes and suffixes. Here's an exercise from lesson 104.

For each word, underline the prefix. Circle the root. Make a line over the suffix.

1. return   4. brightness
2. baker   5. disappear
3. superclean   6. recliner

Other Writing, Grammar and Comprehension Topics

In additon to the three main tracks above, the Language Arts Guide develops skills on the following topics: subject-verb agreement, word usage, taking notes, outlining, discriminating fact and opinion, analyzing similes and idioms, identifying synonyms and opposites. Also, the guide presents 16 writing exercises. Some require narrative writing (writing an interesting story based on a picture), others require an "essay" on specific topics, (for example, My Favorite Animal) and others require writing verse.

APPENDIX A–PLACEMENT

Administering the Placement Test

As a rule of thumb, students who have successfully completed *Reading Mastery Plus* Level 2 or a second grade reading program should be able to succeed in *Reading Mastery Plus* Level 3. However, this rule may not apply to all students, particularly those who can decode words silently but cannot read aloud with sufficient accuracy (no more than two errors per hundred words). Also, students who are extremely weak in answering written comprehension questions should not go into *Reading Mastery Plus* Level 3.

The reproducible Placement Test on page 88 determines the rate-accuracy and comprehension performance of students. Administer the test to all students before placing them in the program. The test results will provide you with:

- "baseline" information about students' reading rate and accuracy

- a basis for evaluating their improvement after they have completed the program

- a means of identifying students who may be placed in the program "on trial," and those who should not be placed in the program.

Part 1 of the test consists of eleven vocabulary words and a reading passage. The vocabulary word-reading is not scored. The reading passage contains 159 words and is timed and scored.

Part 1 of the test is to be administered individually to the students. They should not observe others taking the test. Part 1 requires about two and a half minutes per student. You will need a **stop watch.**

Part 2 of the test may be presented to all students at the same time. Part 2 requires the students to write answers to comprehension questions about the Part 1 passage. Students have 2 minutes to complete Part 2.

Instructions for Part 1

Reproduce the Placement Test that appears on page 88. Make one copy for each student that you are to test. Then follow these steps:

1. Call a student to a corner of the room, where the test will be given.

2. Show a copy of the test to the student.

Part 1 Vocabulary Reading

- (Teacher reference:)

1. **expert**	7. **difference**
2. **clinic**	8. **mirror**
3. **interest**	9. **through**
4. **changes**	10. **practicing**
5. **themselves**	11. **questions**
6. **people**	

3. Point to the column of words at the top of the test. Tell the student: Touch word 1. (Wait.) That word is **expert.**

4. Repeat step 3 for words 2–11.

5. Your turn to read those words.

6. Word 1. What word?

7. Repeat step 6 for words 2–11.

Part 1 Passage Reading

8. Point to the passage in Part 1.

9. Tell the student: You're going to read this passage out loud. I want you to read it as well as you can. Don't try to read it so fast that you make mistakes. But don't read it so slowly that it doesn't make any sense. You have two minutes to read the passage. Go.

10. Time the student. If the student takes more than three seconds on a word, say the word, count it as an error, and permit the student to continue reading. To record errors, make one tally mark for each error.

Count all the following behaviors as errors:

• Misreading a word (Count as one error.)

• Omitting a word part (Count as one error.)

• Skipping a word (Count as one error.)

• Skipping a line (Immediately show the student the correct line. Count as one error.)

• Not identifying a word within three seconds (Tell the word. Count as one error.)

Also count each word not read by the end of the two-minute time limit as an error. For example, if the student is eight words from the end of the passage by the end of the time limit, count eight errors.

11. Collect the test sheet.

After you've administered Part 1 to all the students, present Part 2, which is a group test. Administer Part 2 no more than 2 hours after students complete Part 1. Here are the steps to follow:

1. Assemble the students.

2. Give each student a copy of the placement test.

3. Give the group these instructions: At the bottom of the page are questions about the passage that you read earlier. Write the answers. You have two minutes to finish.

4. Time the students. Collect the test sheets after two minutes.

Answer Key   Part 2

1. What was the first name of the man in the story? _____ **Bill** _____

2. Underline 4 things he did to try to be more interesting.
   • frown more
   • <u>smile more</u>
   • whisper
   • <u>ask questions</u>
   • answer questions
   • <u>talk louder</u>
   • talk softer
   • <u>talk faster</u>
   • talk slower

3. His problem was that he
   • was old
   • had five dogs
   • <u>put people to sleep</u>

4. He practiced in front of
   • his wife
   • <u>the mirror</u>
   • the TV

5. Who came over when he was practicing?

   • a sleeper   • a dog expert

            • <u>a sleep expert</u>

6. Name the place where she worked.

   <u>Sleep More Clinic</u>

Placement Criteria

Use the table below to determine placement for each student.

Errors	Placement
If a student makes 7 errors or more on Part 1 **OR** 2 errors or more on Part 2	Place the student in a reading-language program more elementary than *Reading Mastery Plus* Level 3, possibly *Reading Mastery Plus* Level 1 or Level 2.
If a student makes no more than 6 errors on Part 1 **AND** no more than 1 error on Part 2.	Place the student at *Reading Mastery Plus* Level 3, lesson 1.

Remedies

The performance on the test shows whether students are weak in decoding or comprehension. Their performance may also imply remedies.

• If students fail Part 1, they are weak in decoding. The simplest remedy for these students is to select material that they are able to read without making more than about two errors per hundred words. Set rate criterion for these students (based on the rate at which they are able to read making no more than two errors per hundred words) and as they improve, change the criterion so they are required to read faster. Continue to provide ample practice until the students read at the minimum rate of 90 words per minute without making more than two errors per hundred words.

• If students fail Part 2, provide practice on basic comprehension questions (who, what, when, where, why). Direct these students to read aloud. Ask questions after each sentence. Make sure that each question can be clearly answered by the passage that the students read. Provide this kind of practice until the students are proficient at answering questions.

Retesting

When you feel that students are firm on skills that were initially deficient, readminister the Placement Test. If students fail a second time, they should be placed, if possible, in a more elementary program.

Bill tried to say things that would interest other people. He asked questions and tried to get people to talk about themselves. He said things that were funny. He talked faster and louder. He tried to smile more when he talked. But all those changes made no difference. After Bill was through speaking, everybody else was sleeping.

One day, Bill was at home. He was practicing in front of the mirror. He smiled, moved around a lot, and talked to the mirror.

Just then the door bell rang. Bill opened the door and saw a woman who said, "I am an expert at making people sleep. I work for the Sleep More Clinic. We help people who have trouble sleeping. I hear that you can make people sleep, too."

"Yes," Bill said. "If I speak for a while, people will sleep."

"That is interesting," the sleep expert said. "Can you explain why people sleep?"

"Yes, I can," Bill said.

Part 1

1. expert
2. clinic
3. interest
4. changes
5. themselves
6. people
7. difference
8. mirror
9. through
10. practicing
11. questions

Part 2

1. What was the first name of the man in the story?

2. Underline 4 things he did to try to be more interesting.

- frown more
- smile more
- whisper
- ask questions
- answer questions

- talk louder
- talk softer
- talk faster
- talk slower

3. His problem was that he

- was old • had five dogs • put people to sleep

4. He practiced in front of

- his wife • the mirror • the TV

5. Who came over when he was practicing?

- a sleeper • a dog expert • a sleep expert

6. Name the place where she worked. _____

APPENDIX B—SPECIAL PROJECTS

PROJECT	PRESENT AFTER LESSON	MATERIALS
Map of Four Mile Lake	23	Large sheet of butcher paper or poster board (at least 5 feet x 4 feet), colored marker, scissors, construction paper, possibly paints or crayons, paste
Experiment of water's skin	35	Steel wool (preferably without soap), a transparent bowl, water, and several steel objects, like a wrench, screw or nails
Globe of Earth	52	Large plastic beachball (at least 18 inches in diameter), scissors, paste or tape, construction paper, colored markers, possibly crayons or paint
Illustrate an island sunset	61	Drawing paper and crayons, markers or paints
Model of machine to pull a fish net out of the water	63	Cardboard tube from a roll of paper towels, a short pencil (for handle), four long pencils (for struts), cheesecloth, string or plants that can be woven into a vine, four or more small plastic fish, rubber bands, shallow pan, modeling clay, water
Shipwrecked song		Optional: accompaniment instrument for the tune "On Top of Old Smoky"
Trojan War play	67	A card table, bedsheets or something else to cover the table, butcher paper, and props such as chairs or tables to make the wall of Troy
How good is a dog's nose?	78	Paper and pencil to write questions and take notes. To find answers to some of the questions, students may need to use CD-ROMs
Research Greek myths	81	Research source materials (dictionaries, encyclopedias, CD-ROMs)
Football display	106	Reference materials on football and poster-making supplies (butcher paper or poster board, markers, crayons, paints, scissors, paste, magazines for pictures)
Animals of Australia	122	Reference materials (Australia books, animal books, encyclopedias, CD-ROMs) and poster-making supplies (butcher paper or poster board, markers, crayons, paints, scissors, paste, magazines for pictures)
Word game	127	Cardstock paper cut into "cards"
Research famous Vikings	143	Biographies of Leif Ericson and Eric the Red
Research George Washington	144	Biography of George Washington
Time line	145	Large butcher paper or poster board (at least 2 feet by 5 feet), markers, crayons, paints, scissors, and other construction materials
Interview		Globe

APPENDIX C—MODEL VOCABULARY SENTENCES

LESSON INTRODUCED	SENTENCE NUMBER	SENTENCE
4	1	You measure your weight in pounds.
7	2	They waded into the stream to remove tadpoles.
11	3	The fly boasted about escaping from the spider.
14	4	The workers propped up the cage with steel bars.
17	5	Hunters were stationed at opposite ends of the field.
25	6	He motioned to the flight attendant ahead of him.
29	7	The traffic was moving forty miles per hour.
33	8	He is supposed to make a decision in a couple of days.
37	9	Several paths continued for a great distance.
41	10	Boiling water will thaw ice in a few moments.
45	11	They were eager to hear the announcement.
48	12	The lifeboat disappeared in the whirlpool.
52	13	The smoke swirled in enormous billows.
55	14	The occasional foul smell was normal.
58	15	They constructed an enormous machine.
62	16	She survived until she was rescued.
65	17	The soldiers protected their equipment.
68	18	Lawyers with talent normally succeed.
72	19	A dozen typists approached the stairs.
76	20	The job required a consultant.
81	21	The adults huddled around the fire.
87	22	The customer bought a valuable gift.
91	23	They had reasons for interrupting her talk.
95	24	He frequently argued about the championship.
101	25	She commented about the still water.
107	26	Their amazing effort surprised the neighbors.
111	27	Police officers checked the ship's cargo.
115	28	The champions performed perfectly.
118	29	She paid the correct amount.
122	30	Perhaps they will reply in a few days.
127	31	The palace guards spoke different languages.
131	32	His argument convinced them to buy an appliance.
138	33	The army was soundly defeated near the village.

APPENDIX D–STUDENT GLOSSARY

adults   *Adults* are grown-ups.

adventure   When you have an *adventure*, you do something very exciting.

ahead   *Ahead* is another word for *in front*.

Alaska   *Alaska* is the largest state.

allow   When you *allow* somebody to do something, you permit that person to do it.

although   In some sentences, *although* is another word for *but*.

amazing   Something that is *amazing* is very hard to believe.

America   *America* is a large part of the world.

amount   The *amount* of something tells how much there is.

ancient   Things that are *ancient* are very, very old.

animal preserve   An *animal preserve* is a place that protects animals.

ankles   Your *ankles* are the joints right above your feet.

announce   When you *announce* something, you let others know about it.

announcement   An *announcement* is a message.

apart   Things that are not close to each other are far *apart*.

appear   When something first comes into sight, it *appears*.

appliances   *Appliances* are machines that are used around the house.

approach   When you *approach* something, you move toward it.

argue   When you *argue* with someone, you tell why you don't agree with what that person says.

argument   An *argument* is what you say to make people believe you.

army   An *army* is the group of people that goes to war for a country.

arrange   When things are *arranged*, the things are in place.

ashamed   When you feel *ashamed*, you feel that you've done something bad.

ashes   The stuff that is left over after something burns up is called *ashes*.

at bat   When a person is *at bat* in a baseball game, that person has a turn at hitting the ball.

attach   Something that is *attached* is connected.

attack   When people *attack*, they do something to start a fight or a battle.

attention   When something catches your *attention*, you know it's there.

Australia   *Australia* is the name of a country.

awful   Something that is *awful* is very bad.

battered   When something is *battered*, it is beaten up.

battle   A *battle* in a war is one of the smaller fights that takes place in the war.

before long   If something happens very soon, it happens *before long*.

behave   The way you *behave* is the way you act.

beyond a doubt   When you know something *beyond a doubt*, you know it for sure.

billows   *Billows* are large clouds or waves that are swelling up.

binoculars   *Binoculars* are powerful glasses that make far-off things look close.

blade   The *blade* is the flat part of a tool that is connected to a handle.

blame   When you say that things went wrong because of somebody else, you *blame* that person.

block   When you *block* in a football game, you push a player from the other team without using your hands to grab the player.

boast   *Boast* is another word for *brag*.

boil   When water *boils*, it makes lots of bubbles and steam.   Water boils at 212 degrees.

boiled   Things that are *boiled* are cooked in bubbling hot water.

booms   When a voice *booms*, it's very loud.

bow (rhymes with *how*)   The *bow* is the front of a ship.

bow (rhymes with *how*)   When you *bow*, you bend forward.

broiled Things that are *broiled* are cooked over an open fire.

buried When something is *buried*, it has things piled on top of it.

calm When things are *calm*, they are very quiet and peaceful.

Canada *Canada* is one of the countries of America.

captain The *captain* of a ship or plane is the person in charge of the vehicle.

cargo *Cargo* is what ships carry from one place to another.

catch your breath When you *catch your breath*, you breathe very hard.

cave A *cave* is a hole in the ground that is big enough for people or animals to go into.

center The *center* of something is the middle of the thing.

centimeters *Centimeters* are used to tell how long things are. There are 100 centimeters in a meter.

certain *Certain* is another word for *sure*.

championship A *championship* is a contest between the two best teams.

character A *character* is a person or animal in a story.

charge When an animal *charges*, it puts its head down and runs at something as fast as it can go.

Chicago *Chicago* is a large city near the middle of the United States.

chilled When you feel cold, you feel *chilled*.

China *China* is a large country near Japan.

claim When you *claim* something, you say it's yours.

clomping A *clomping* sound is the sound a horse makes when it walks on a street.

clue *Clues* are hints.

coach A *coach* is the person who gives orders to the players on a team.

coast The *coast* is where the land meets the ocean.

cock your head When you *cock your head*, you tilt it.

coconuts *Coconuts* are fruits with heavy shells.

Columbus The name of the man who sailed across the

ocean and discovered America is *Columbus*.

comfortable When something feels *comfortable*, it feels pretty good.

comment When you *comment* about something, you quickly tell about that thing.

complaint A *complaint* is a statement that tells what you don't like about something.

completely *Completely* is another word for *totally*.

computer *Computers* are machines that you can use to work problems and play games.

Concord *Concord* is the name of one of the first towns in the United States.

confusion When things are very strange and mixed up, we say things are thrown into *confusion*.

constantly Things that go on *constantly* go on all the time.

construct When you *construct* something, you *build* it.

consultant A *consultant* is a person who is hired for a special job.

contest Any game or event that has winners and losers is a *contest*.

continue If something *continues*, it keeps on going.

convince When you *convince* people, you make them believe something.

copilot A *copilot* is the person who works with the pilot in flying the plane.

correct *Correct* is another word for *right*.

cottonwood *Cottonwood* trees are large trees.

count on When you can be sure of something, you can *count on* that thing.

couple A *couple* of things is two things.

crate A *crate* is a wooden box that is used to ship things.

creek A *creek* is a small stream.

crouch When you *crouch*, you bend close to the ground.

current *Currents* are places where water is moving.

customer A person who buys things at a store is a *customer* of that store.

damage If you do *damage* to something, you break part of it or ruin it.

danger   When you're in a place where you could get hurt, you're in *danger* of getting hurt.

dates   *Dates* are small sweet fruits that grow on some palm trees.

daydream   When you *daydream*, you think of nice things that you would like to happen.

deaf   People who are *deaf* cannot hear anything.

decision   When you make a *decision* to do something, you make up your mind to do it.

defeat   *Defeated* is another word for *beaten*.

degrees   You measure temperature in *degrees*.

demand   When you *demand* an answer, you insist on it.

Denver   *Denver* is a large city about halfway between Chicago and San Francisco.

describe   When you *describe* something, you tell how it looks or how it works.

destroy   If you ruin something so it can't be fixed, you *destroy* that thing.

direct   Things that are *direct* are straight and simple.

disappear   When something *disappears*, you can't see it anymore.

discover   The person who is the first to find something is the person who *discovers* that thing.

distance   The farther apart things are, the bigger the *distance* between them.

double   *Double* means *two times as much*.

dozen   *Dozen* is another word for *twelve*.

drifts   When something *drifts*, *winds or currents make it move slowly*.

dull   Things that are boring are *dull*.

during   If something happens *during* the night, it happens while the night is going on.

eager   When you're *eager* for something, you are really looking forward to it.

earlier   Something that happens *earlier* happens before another thing.

earplugs   *Earplugs* are rubber things that you stick in your ears.   It is hard to hear when you are wearing earplugs.

earth   *Earth* is another name for our world.

earth   *Earth* is another word for *dirt*.

earthquake   When an *earthquake* takes place, the ground moves and shakes and splits open.

echo   When you hear an *echo,* you hear a sound that is repeated.

effort   Something that takes a lot of strength takes a lot of *effort.*

Egypt   *Egypt* is the name of a country.

electric   Things that are *electric* run on electricity, not on fuel.

electricity   *Electricity* is the power you get when you plug things into wall outlets.

encyclopedia   An *encyclopedia* is a large set of books that gives information about anything you can name.

engine   The *engine* of a vehicle is the part that makes the vehicle run.

England   *England* is a country that is almost 4 thousand miles from the United States.

English   *English* is the name of the language that people speak in England and the United States.

enormous   *Enormous* means *very, very large.*

eohippus   *Eohippus* is the first kind of horse that lived on Earth.

equipment   Large machines and tools are called *equipment.*

escape   When you *escape* from something, you get away from it.

examine   When you *examine* something, you look at it closely.

except   *Except* is another word for *but* in some sentences.

excitement   When you are worked up and have trouble sitting still, you feel *excitement.*

exit   When you *exit* a place, you leave the place.

expensive   Things that cost a lot of money are *expensive.*

explain   When you *explain* something, you give information about that thing.

expression   The *expression* on your face shows what you're feeling.

facts   Sentences that give you information are *facts*.

fades   When something *fades*, it slowly disappears.

fail   The opposite of *succeed* is *fail*.

faint   When you *faint*, you pass out.

famous   If something is *famous*, it is *well-known*.

fancy   If an office is *fancy*, it is not plain.

fear   If you *fear* something, you are afraid of it.

field goal   A *field goal* is a score in football that is made by kicking the ball.

figure out   When you *figure out* something, you learn it.

finally   *Finally* means *at last*.

finest   Something that is the *finest* is the most expensive or the best.

fire dies down   When a *fire dies down*, it doesn't go out.

fired   When you are *fired* from a job, you are told you can't work at that job anymore.

first base   *First base* is the first base you run to after you hit the ball in a game of baseball.

flight attendant   A *flight attendant* is somebody who works on a plane and takes care of passengers.

force   A *force* is a *push*.

forever   If something lasts *forever*, it never never ends.

foul   *Foul* is another word for *bad*.

frequently   *Frequently* is another word for *often*.

frisky   *Frisky* means *playful* or *full of energy*.

fronds   *Fronds* are the branches of palm trees.

frost   *Frost* is frozen water that forms on grass during cold nights.

fuel   *Fuel* is what engines burn when they run.

gain   When a ball carrier goes the right way in football, he makes a *gain*. When he gets tackled before he can make a gain, he makes a loss.

galley   The *galley* is the kitchen on a plane or ship.

garden   A *garden* is a place where you grow flowers or vegetables.

gift   A *gift* is another way of saying a *present*.

globe   A small model of Earth is called a *globe*.

glows   When something *glows*, it gives off light.

go out for a team   When you *go out for a team*, you show the coach how good you are.

grain   *Grain* is the seed of grass or cereal plants.

gram   A *gram* is a very small unit of weight.

graph   A *graph* is a kind of a picture that has lines or parts that show different amounts.

great   *Great* is another word for *wonderful*.

Greece   *Greece* is the name of a country.

groceries   The food that you buy at the supermarket or grocery store is called *groceries*.

grove   A *grove* of trees is a small group of trees.

guard   A *guard* is a person whose job is to protect something.

gust   A *gust* of wind is a sudden wind that blows for a very short time.

half   If you cut something in *half*, you get two pieces that are the same size. Each piece is half.

half-aware   When you are *half-aware* of something, you are not paying much attention to it.

hallelujah   People who say *"Hallelujah"* are feeling great joy.

harm   *Harm* is another word for *hurt*.

hay   *Hay* is dried grass that horses and cows eat.

heat   When things feel hot, they give off *heat*.

herd   A *herd* of animals is a group of animals that run together.

hoist   When you *hoist* something, you lift it up.

holler   Another word for *holler* is *yell*.

hollow   Something that is *hollow* is not solid.

home run   When a baseball player hits a *home run*, the player hits the ball so far that nobody can get it before the player runs around all four bases.

homonym   A *homonym* is a word that sounds the same as another word.

honest   Here's another way of saying I'm telling the truth: *honest*.

hooves   *Hooves* are the kind of feet that deer and horses and cows have. *Hoof* tells about one foot. *Hooves* tells about more than one foot.

huddle   When people crowd close together, they *huddle*.

human   A *human* is a person.

humans   *Humans* are people.

illegal   Things that are *illegal* are against the law.

imagining   *Imagining* is a kind of thinking.

imitate   When you *imitate* somebody, you do exactly what that person does.

important   If something is *important*, you should pay attention to it.

impression   When you have an *impression* about something, you have an idea about that thing.

in fact   Here's another way of saying that something is true: *in fact*.

India   *India* is a large country on the other side of the world.

insect   An *insect* is a bug that has six legs.

insist   When you keep telling that you want something, you *insist* on that thing.

interrupt   When you *interrupt* somebody, you start talking before the other person finishes.

investigate   When you *investigate* something, you try to learn the facts about that thing.

involved   People who take part in a game are *involved* in the game.

Italy   *Italy* is a country near Greece.

Japan   *Japan* is a country that is 5 thousand miles from the United States.

jewels   *Jewels* are valuable stones.

juggle   When you *juggle* objects, you keep tossing the objects in the air and you make sure that at least two objects are always in the air at the same time.

jungle   A *jungle* is a forest that is always warm and wet.

Kennedy Airport   *Kennedy Airport* is a large airport in New York City.

koala   A *koala* is an animal that looks like a teddy bear and lives in Australia.

lad   A *lad* is a young man.

Lake Michigan   *Lake Michigan* is one of the five Great Lakes.

language   A *language* is the words that people in a country use to say things.

lawn   *Lawn* is the name for grass that is well-kept and mowed.

lawyer   *Lawyers* are people who help us when we have questions about the law.

lean   Something that *leans* does not stand straight up and down.

ledge   A *ledge* is a narrow step that is on cliffs or mountains.

let somebody down   When you *let somebody down*, that person thinks you will help and you don't help.

lifeboats   *Lifeboats* are emergency boats that are on large ships.

lighter   *Lighter* is the opposite of *heavier*.

lookout   A *lookout* is a person who looks in all directions to see if trouble is near.

loss   When a ball carrier goes the right way in football, he makes a gain. When he gets tackled before he can make a gain, he makes a *loss*.

lowered   When something is *lowered*, it is moved down.

machine   A *machine* is something that is made to help people do work.

magnet   A *magnet* is something that hangs on to things made of steel or iron.

magnetic   Things that are *magnetic* stick to a magnet.

make sense   When things don't *make sense* to you, they are not at all clear to you.

make-believe   *Make-believe* is another word for *pretend*.

manage   When you have to work hard to do something, you *manage* to do it.

mean   When you do what you *mean* to do, you do what you plan to do.

measure   When you *measure* something, you find out how long it is or how hot it is or how heavy it is or how tall it is.

mention   When you tell just a little bit about something, you *mention* that thing.

Mexico   *Mexico* is one of the countries of America.

microphone   A *microphone* is a tool that picks up sounds.

million   A *million* is a very, very large number.

million   A *million* is one thousand thousand.

modern   *Modern* is the opposite of *old-fashioned*.

moist   Things that are *moist* are slightly wet, not dripping wet.

moments   A few *moments* is not very many seconds.

motion   When you *motion* to another person, you use your hands or body to show the person what to do.

mumble   When you *mumble*, you talk to yourself so others can't understand everything you say.

mummy   One kind of *mummy* is a dead person all wrapped up in strips of cloth.

muscle   *Muscles* are the meaty parts of your body that make your body move.

myna   A *myna* is a bird.

neighbors   *Neighbors* are people who live near you or sit near you.

New York City   *New York City* is the name of one of the largest cities in the world.

normal   *Normal* is another word for *usual*.

normally   *Normally* is another word for *usually*.

object   When you argue that something is wrong, you *object* to that thing.

occasional   *Occasional* means *once in a while*.

ocean   An *ocean* is a very large body of salt water.

offer   When you *offer* something, you give someone a chance to take it.

Ohio   *Ohio* is a state between Chicago and New York.

open field   An *open field* is a place with just grass and no trees.

opposite   Hot is the *opposite* of cold.

outcome   The *outcome* of an event is the way things turn out.

Pacific Ocean   The *Pacific Ocean* is the ocean that borders the west coast of the United States.

packed   When things are squeezed into a small space, they are *packed*.

palace   A king and queen live in a *palace*.   A *palace* is a very large and fancy place.

panel   A flat part that's shaped like a rectangle is called a *panel*.

passenger   A *passenger* is someone who rides in a vehicle.

peacock   A *peacock* is a very large bird with beautiful feathers.

peek   When you sneak a quick look at something, you *peek*.

peel   Another name for the skin of an orange is the *peel* of an orange.

per   *Per* means *each*.

perfect   Something that is *perfect* has everything just the way it should be.

perfectly   If you do something *perfectly*, you don't make any mistakes.

perform   When you *perform*, you put on a show.

perhaps   *Perhaps* is another word for *maybe*.

permit   When you *let* people do something, you *permit* them to do it.

poison   If *poison* gets inside your body, it will make your body stop working and it may kill you.

police officers   *Police officers* are cops.

poster   A *poster* is a large picture that tells about something.

pouch   A *pouch* is a small bag that holds things.

pounds   *Pounds* are a unit used to measure weight.

practice   Things that you *practice* are things that you do again and again.

preserve   When you *preserve* something, you save it or protect it.

president   The *president* of a country is the person who has the most power to run that country.

pretend   When you *pretend* to do something, you make-believe.

probably   If something will *probably* happen, you are pretty sure it will happen.

professional football league
A *professional football league* is a group of teams that play football.

project A *project* is a large job.

prop up When you *prop up* something, you support the thing so it will stay in place.

protect When you *protect* something, you make sure that nothing can hurt it.

prove When you *prove* something, you show that it is true.

puzzled Another word for *confused* is *puzzled*.

pyramid A *pyramid* is a type of building found in Egypt.

queen Usually, a *queen* is the wife of a king.

raft A *raft* is a flat boat.

ramp A *ramp* is a walkway that goes uphill.

raw Food that is not cooked is *raw*.

realize When you *realize* something, you suddenly understand if for the first time.

reason When you tell why you do something, you give a *reason* for doing that thing.

receive When somebody gives you something, you *receive* it.

recognize When you *recognize* something that you see or feel, you know what it is.

record Somebody who sets a *record* does something better than anybody has done before.

referee A *referee* is a person who makes decisions about how a game is played.

refund When your money is *refunded*, it is returned.

relatives Your *relatives* are people in your family.

remain *Remain* is another word for *slay*.

remove When you *remove* something, you get rid of it or take it away.

reply *Reply* is another word for *answer*.

report When you give a *report*, you give the facts.

required Things that are *required* are needed.

rescue Somebody who is *rescued* is *saved* from some kind of danger.

respond When you *respond* to someone, you answer that person.

rich   If you have lots and lots of money, you are *rich*.

rip-off   A *rip-off* is a bad deal.

rise   *Rise* is another word for *moves up*.

roadside   A *roadside* business is a business that is alongside the road.

ruin   When you *ruin* something, you destroy it or do something to it so it won't work.

rule   A *rule* tells you what to do.

ruler   A *ruler* is a tool that you use to measure inches or centimeters.

runway   A *runway* is like a large road that airplanes use when they take off.

rushing   *Rushing* is another word for *moving fast*.

Russia   *Russia* is the name of a very large country.

salesperson   A person who sells things is a *salesperson*.

San Francisco   *San Francisco* is a city on the west coast of the United States.

scales   The skin of fish is covered with *scales*.

scar   A *scar* is a mark left from a bad cut or burn.

screech   A *screech* is a high, sharp sound.

scold   When your mother *scolds* you, she lets you know what you did wrong.

seasons   Each year has four *seasons*: spring, summer, fall, winter.

sense   Another word for a *feeling* is a *sense*.

service   People who offer a *service* do a special job.

several   *Several* things are more than two things but less than many things.

shabby   Something that is *shabby* is not neat and clean.

shallow   *Shallow* is the opposite of *deep*.

show up   When you go to a place, you *show up* at that place.

skeleton   An animal's *skeleton* is all the bones of the animal's body.

slave   A *slave* is a person who has very few rights.

slight   Something that is *slight* is not very big.

smooth and quiet   When things are *smooth and quiet*, they are very calm.

soldiers   *Soldiers* are men and women in the army.

soundly   *Soundly* means *completely* or *really*.

Spain   *Spain* is a country that is near Italy.

sped   *Sped* is another word for *went fast*.

speedometer   A *speedometer* is the dial in a vehicle that shows how fast the vehicle is moving.

spices   *Spices* are things that you add to food to give it a special flavor.

spoiled   *Spoiled* children cry and act like babies to make people do things for them.

spy   A *spy* is a person who gives important information to the enemy.

stale   Food that is *stale* is old and not very good to eat.

stands   The *stands* in a ball park are the seats where people sit.

stars   The best players are called *stars*.

starve   When people have no food to eat for a long time, they *starve*.

stationed   When someone is *stationed* in a place, the person is supposed to stay in that place.

steel   *Steel* is a very tough metal.

stern   The *stern* is the back of a ship.

still   Another word for *silent* or *peaceful* is *still*.

strange   If something looks *strange*, it does not look like you think it should look.

strength   Your *strength* is how strong you are.

stretch   When things *stretch* out, they are very wide or very long.

striped   If something is *striped*, it has stripes.

strut   *Strutting* is a kind of show-off walking.

succeed   When you *succeed* at something, you do it the way you planned.

sunken ship   A *sunken ship* is a ship at the bottom of the ocean.

support   When you *support* something, you hold it up or hold it in place.

supposed to   *Supposed to* means *should*.

survive   When you *survive*, you manage to stay alive.

swirl   When something *swirls*, it spins around as it drifts.

swoop   Things that *swoop* move in big curves.

tackle   When you *tackle* players in football, you bring them down so their knees hit the ground.

tadpoles   *Tadpoles* are baby toads or frogs.

takeoff   When an airplane first leaves the ground, it's called the *takeoff*.

talent   People with *talent* are people with special skills.

tame   *Tame* is the opposite of *wild*.

temperature   When you measure the *temperature* of something, you find out how hot it is.

Texas   *Texas* is the second-largest state in the United States.

thaw   *Thaw* means *melt*.

thought   Something that you think about is a *thought*.

thousand   A *thousand* is equal to ten hundreds.

time   When you *time* something, you use a watch to figure out how long it takes.

ton   A *ton* is two thousand pounds.

touchdown   When you score a *touchdown* in football, you take the ball across the goal line.

traffic   All the vehicles that are driving on a street are the *traffic*.

treasure   *Treasures* are things that are worth a lot of money.

triple   *Triple* means *three times as much*.

trumpeting   A *trumpeting* sound is something that sounds like it comes from a musical instrument called a trumpet.

trunk   The *trunk* of a tree is the main part that comes out of the ground.

tumbles   When something *tumbles*, it turns over and over.

Turkey   *Turkey* is a country near Egypt.

tusks   The *tusks* of an animal are huge teeth that stick out of the animal's mouth.

twig   A *twig* is a tiny branch.

typist   *Typists* are people who type things very neatly.

uneasy   When you feel nervous, you feel *uneasy*.

unfair   If rules are not the same for everybody, the rules are *unfair*.

unpleasant   Things that are *unpleasant* are not nice.

usually   Things that *usually* happen are things that happen most of the time.

valuable   Things that are worth a lot of money are *valuable*.

Viking   The *Vikings* were people who lived long ago and sailed to many parts of the world.

village   A *village* is a small town.

wade   When you *wade*, you walk in water that is not very deep.

war   A *war* is a long fight between two countries.

warn   When you *warn* people, you let them know that trouble is near.

warts   *Warts* are little bumps that some people have on their body. Toads have warts, too.

water strider   A *water strider* is an insect that can walk on the top of water.

we'd   *We'd* is a contraction for the words *we would* or *we had*.

weak   *Weak* means *not strong*.

weather   When you tell about the *weather*, you tell about the temperature, the wind, the clouds, and if it is raining or snowing.

weigh   When you measure how many grams or pounds something is, you *weigh* it.

weight   The *weight* of an object is how heavy that object is.

well   A *well* is a deep hole in the ground.

weren't   *Weren't* is a contraction for the words *were not*.

whirlpool   The water in a *whirlpool* goes around and around as it goes down.

whole   *Whole* means all of it—the whole thing.

wise   Someone who is *wise* is very smart.

worth   Something is *worth* the amount of money people would pay for it.

worthless   Something that is *worthless* is not worth anything.

woven   Things made of cloth are *woven*.

wrap   When you *wrap* a package with paper, you put paper around it.

yard   A *yard* tells how long things are. A yard is almost as long as a meter.

almost 18	boy 69	clay 21	darker 124
almost 17	boys 71	clean 31	darker 129
also 17	brag 1	clean 32	deal 26
also 25	brand 1	clean 34	deal 93
always 132	brick 42	cleaned 49	dearly 107
always 107	brick 31	cleaner 119	deck 29
always 22	broiler 73	cleaner 55	dime 96
always 19	broken 129	cleanest 51	diving 123
another 145	broken 132	cleaning 45	doll 57
anybody 136	brushed 68	cleaning 101	downtown 144
anyone 135	bull 58	cleans 37	draw 82
anything 136	cake 99	cleans 43	dream 91
arms 18	camp 4	clearly 51	dream 26
awful 123	camper 119	clearly 83	dreamer 44
awful 83	campfire 138	clearly 108	dreaming 106
bake 87	camping 78	closed 124	dreams 38
bald 19	card 18	closer 128	drip 11
ball 57	careless 103	cloud 33	driver 115
barn 17	champ 6	clouds 41	drooping 77
barns 39	champ 8	coiled 71	drop 22
baseball 139	charm 17	coin 68	dropped 113
bath 7	charming 59	cold 23	drops 39
bathroom 144	charming 45	colder 45	dull 56
beach 27	chart 19	coldest 51	dulled 75
beach 41	chart 18	coldest 74	dullest 64
beam 28	cheap 26	cone 86	eaten 124
became 137	cheap 35	cowboy 139	everyone 135
become 138	cheap 59	cramp 3	everything 136
bedroom 138	cheap 91	cramp 1	fall 94
bells 62	cheaper 47	crash 36	fallen 128
bend 2	cheapest 53	crash 7	falling 73
beside 137	cheapest 68	crash 42	fanning 113
bike 86	cheaply 84	crash 9	farm 25
bike 94	cheaply 54	crashed 61	farmer 44
biker 113	chest 11	crashed 69	farming 54
bite 89	chest 8	crashed 48	farms 39
bitten 129	chill 57	crashing 79	farms 37
blast 13	chin 34	crawl 81	fast 4
blond 22	chin 9	crawling 104	fastest 83
boil 67	chin 28	crawling 83	fastest 52
boiled 105	chin 7	crawling 108	fatten 131
boiler 71	chop 14	cream 36	fatter 123
boiling 74	chosen 127	crop 1	fawn 82
bone 87	clapping 121	crop 15	fear 27
boot 94	claw 95	cupful 52	fell 58
booted 77	clawed 84	damp 12	file 89
boots 107	clawing 105	dampen 104	fill 61
boy 67	claws 81	darken 105	fine 94

fine 85	handful 101	lend 3	onto 137
fireside 139	handful 65	licked 112	ouch 33
fish 16	handful 131	life 92	out 32
fished 111	harden 127	lifeboat 142	outcome 142
fishing 48	harden 107	lifeless 103	outfit 142
fishing 63	harden 131	lifetime 142	outside 138
flame 86	harmful 51	like 95	outsmart 142
flames 115	hawk 81	liked 112	overtime 143
flaming 122	hawks 133	liked 128	pills 64
flash 16	helpful 69	lime 91	planning 126
flash 5	hint 13	limp 4	plant 36
flatly 79	hoist 125	line 85	plant 3
flatten 132	hoist 66	line 96	planted 44
flatten 127	hold 35	locks 37	planter 63
flatten 114	hold 24	loop 76	plants 41
flip 1	holder 72	looping 77	plants 37
fold 23	holder 121	loosen 127	plants 48
fold 34	holding 47	lump 22	play 19
folder 48	holds 37	made 85	played 133
folder 111	hole 97	make 94	player 54
fond 16	home 96	makes 113	player 49
fondly 73	home 85	march 21	players 59
fooler 79	homeless 103	math 5	playful 75
football 141	hoop 76	may 19	playful 52
footprint 141	hope 97	meal 43	playful 65
forever 141	hoped 121	meal 27	playful 108
fork 24	hopeful 104	meal 92	playful 111
form 34	hopeless 114	meals 99	playing 115
form 25	hopeless 102	meanest 65	plays 38
form 23	hopes 109	meanest 52	plays 42
forms 42	hoping 133	mile 87	point 68
forms 38	hoping 126	mill 59	pointed 105
found 32	hound 93	mine 86	pointer 75
found 92	however 139	mine 93	pointing 71
fresh 13	hush 16	moist 68	pond 14
fresh 16	inside 138	moist 66	pray 21
fresh 9	inside 145	mold 41	print 1
freshen 102	into 137	mold 28	pull 59
freshest 134	jaw 81	mole 101	pulled 99
freshly 126	joined 72	moons 78	pulling 62
full 58	joined 109	mouthful 55	rake 101
fuller 65	joking 121	mouthful 84	ranch 5
fuller 106	joy 66	much 15	raw 82
fullest 63	joyful 71	must 15	reach 27
game 98	killer 75	must 14	reach 96
games 108	kite 98	neck 31	rested 119
given 131	lake 95	necks 41	restful 53
given 129	lamps 69	nine 91	restless 105
gold 25	lamps 38	nobody 136	restless 102
golden 103	last 2	nobody 135	rock 29
golden 132	lasted 127	nose 97	room 76
goldfish 141	law 82	oil 67	roomful 83
gulls 61	leaf 33	olden 104	rooming 77
hand 2	leafless 104	older 133	rope 89
handed 46	leap 91	oldest 79	roped 131
handful 51	leaps 38	oldest 112	round 33

Spelling Word List

APPENDIX F—READING SELECTIONS

LESSON NUMBER	COMPREHENSION PASSAGE	MAIN STORY TITLE
1	*Living Things*	The Tiger and the Frog
2	*Make-Believe Animals*	Bob and Don Find Moops
3	*Trees*	Don Washes the White Spot
4	*Apple Trees*	The Little Apple Tree
5	*Forest Fires*	Campers Come into the Forest
6	*Camels and Pigs*	Tina Is Happy
7	*More Facts About Camels*	The Camel and the Pig
8	*Facts About Centimeters*	The Camel and the Pig Trade Parts
9	*Felt-Tipped Pens*	Joe Williams Wants a New Job
11	*Centimeters*	Joe Williams Gets a New Job
12	*Facts About Fleas*	Aunt Fanny's Flea Circus
13	*1) Learning About Time* *2) Facts About Flea Circuses*	The Fleas Surprise Aunt Fanny
14	*1) Meters* *2) Directions on a Map*	Aunt Fanny Changes Her Ways
15	*Facts About Toads and Frogs*	Goad the Toad
16	*More Facts About Toads and Frogs*	Goad Uses Her First Trick
17	*1) How Far Apart Things Are* *2) How Toads Catch Flies*	Food Traps
18	*1) Facts About Moles* *2) The Opposite Direction*	Goad's Four Tricks
19	*1) Binoculars* *2) How Fast Things Move*	The Brown Family Comes to Catch Goad
21	*1) Animals and Fire* *2) Smoke and Wind*	The Browns Make Up a Plan
22	*1) Names That Tell How Fast Things Move* *2) How Air Moves an Object*	Goad in the Water
23	*Facts About Miles*	A Big Picnic
24	*More Facts About Miles*	Jack and Lisa Have a Race
25	*Telling How Two Things Are Different*	Nancy Wants to Stay Little
26	*Facts About Ants*	A Green Man Visits Nancy
27		Nancy Is Still Tiny
28	*Sugar Shines*	Nancy Finds Something to Eat
29	*1) Water Has a Skin* *2) Facts About Dew*	Nancy Tries to Get Some Water
31	*More About the Skin That Water Has*	Nancy Gets Some Water
32	*Grams*	Nancy Is Hungry Again
33	*More About Grams*	Nancy Finds Some More Food
34		The Green Man Visits Nancy Again
35	*Sounds That Objects Make*	Nancy Becomes Regular Size
36	*Miles Per Hour*	A Push in the Opposite Direction
37	*More About Pushes in the Opposite Direction*	Herman the Fly
38	*Speedometers*	Herman Goes to Kennedy Airport
39	*Airplane Crew Members*	Herman Ends Up on a Jumbo Jet

LESSON NUMBER	COMPREHENSION PASSAGE	MAIN STORY TITLE
41	1) Insects 2) Facts About Speed	Getting Ready for Takeoff
42	Temperature	Herman Takes Off for San Francisco
43	Degrees	Herman Lands in San Francisco
44	Finding the Direction of a Wind	Fly Spray Fills the Air
45	Airplanes and Wind	Rough Air
46	More About the World	Herman Heads to Japan
47	The Eye of a Fly	Herman Tries to Escape
48	1) Facts About Spiders 2) The Size of Some States	The Jumbo Jet Lands in Japan
49		Herman is Cold-Blooded
51	The Air Around The Earth	Herman Flies to Italy
52		Herman's Last Trip
53	1) Facts About Whirlpools 2) Facts About an Ocean Liner 3) Facts About Ocean Water 4) Comparing Things	
54		Linda and Kathy Escape from a Sinking Ship
55	Facts About Islands	Linda and Kathy Find Land
56	Facts About Palm Trees	Alone on an Island
57	Facts About Coconuts	Linda and Kathy Find More Food
58	Facts About Machines	Making Tools
59		Linda and Kathy Construct a Machine
61	Figuring Out the Time of Day	The Girls Have Fish for Dinner
62	Facts About Fevers	Signaling for Help
63	Landing a Ship	The Girls Are Rescued
64	Greece and Troy	Learning About a Time Line
65		The City of Troy
66	When the Story of Troy Took Place	A Great War at Troy
67		The Great Wooden Horse
68		Bertha Has a Great Sense of Smell
69		Maria Gets a Job as an Investigator
71	Oil Wells	Maria Tests Bertha's Talent
72		Maria and Bertha Go to the Oil Refinery
73	Underlined Words	Maria and Bertha Meet Mr. Daniels
74		Bertha Tests Some Water
75		Maria and Bertha Make Up a New Plan
76		Inside a Hot Van
77		The Chief Listens to Bertha
78		Bertha Tests the Water
79	1) Form 50 Special Consultants and Group Leaders 2) Learning About an Achilles Heel	Achilles Heel

LESSON NUMBER	COMPREHENSION PASSAGE	MAIN STORY TITLE
81	Chariots	The Greatest Soldier
82		Clues from Thousands of Years Ago
83		Digging Into Piles
84	Fire and Heat	The Cave People Discover Fire
85		Cave Pictures
86		Different Kinds of Horses
87		Horses from Millions of Years Ago
88		How Horses Changed
89	Filling Out a Bank Form	Andrew Dexter Has Daydreams
91	Learning About Checks	Andrew Visits Magnetic Research Company
92		Andrew Is a Changed Person
93	The Strength of Animals	Andrew Gets Fired
94	Learning About Football	Andrew Meets Denny Brock
95	Seconds	The Titans Make Fun of Andrew
96		Andrew Kicks
97	Professional Football Players	Denny Gives Andrew a Job
98		Andrew Plays in His First Game
99		Andrew Meets Smiling Sam
101		Andrew Begins to Change
102		Andrew Plays Harder
103		The Titans Play Harder
104		Andrew Leaves the Team
105		The Championship Game
106		The End of the Game
107	Places You Have Learned About	Looking for Treasures
108	Words That Talk	Hohoboho
109	Liz Takes a Trip	The Words That Sat in the Back Rows
111	Facts About Canada	The Big Change in Hohoboho
112		Run Gets Moved
113	Facts About Australia	Toby the Kangaroo
114	Facts About Kangaroos	A Job for Toby
115	Facts About Peacocks	The Kangaroo Hunters
116	1) Facts About Minutes 2) Facts About Ships	Toby on the Ship
117		The End of the Trip
118	More Facts About Canada	The Ship Arrives in Canada
119	Facts About a Circus	Toby's New Job
121	Facts About Boxing	Toby Leaves the Circus
122		The Big Fight
123	Homonyms	The Scarred Words in the Word Bank
124	Henry Ouch Takes a Vacation	The Number with the Most Scars
125	A Pilot's Trip	Some Words Stop Fighting
126		Another Change Is Made
127	Contractions	The Last Problem in the Word Bank Is Solved
128	1) Wooden Buildings 2) Time Machines 3) More About a Time Line	
129		Eric and Tom Find a Time Machine

LESSON NUMBER	COMPREHENSION PASSAGE	MAIN STORY TITLE
131	*More About Time*	The San Francisco Earthquake
132	*1) More About Time* *2) Facts About Egypt*	Eric and Tom in Egypt
133	*More About Time*	Eric and Tom Meet the King of Egypt
134	*Inventing*	Eric and Tom Meet the King
135		Eric and Tom Leave Egypt
136	*A Queen Named Helen*	Eric and Tom in Greece
137	*Forty Thousand Years Ago*	Eric and Tom See Cave People
138	*More About Time*	Eric and Tom in the City of the Future
139	*1) More About Time* *2) North America*	Spain in 1492
141	*More About Time*	The Dog and the Time Machine
142	*Vikings*	The Land of the Vikings
143	*More About Time*	Trying to Get Home
144	*Facts About the United States*	Concord
145	*More About Time*	Home

Guide to Reproducible Appendices

2. a. Does dew form in the middle of the day?

    b. Dew forms when the air gets ███.

            • warmer   • cooler   • drier

3. If an ant weighed as much as a cow, the ant could carry an object as heavy as ███.

4. A mile is a little more than ███ feet.

5. Let's say this line ←——→ on the map is 1 mile long
        and this line ←————————→ is 2 miles long.

    a. Say the letter of a line on the map that is 2 miles long.

    b. How far is it from the field to the lake?

    c. How far is it from the park to the forest?

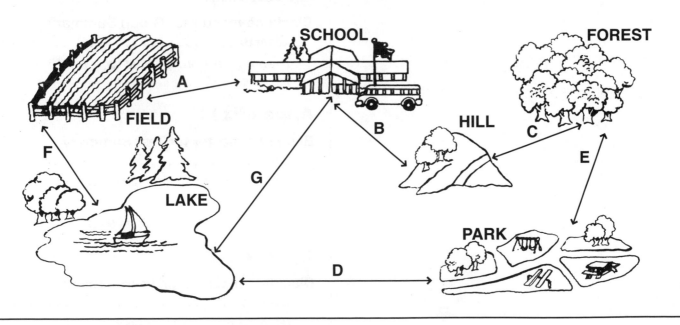

Fact Game

6. What part of the world is shown on the map?

7. One line on the map is 13 hundred miles long. The other line is 25 hundred miles long.

   a. How far is it from J to M?

   b. How far is it from K to P?

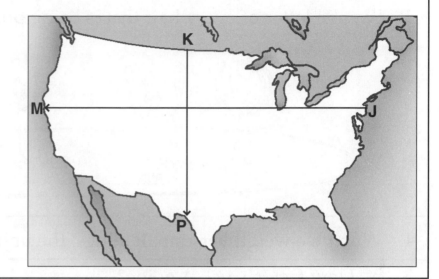

8. Say the part of each name below that tells about time.

   a. inches per week   b. miles per minute   c. meters per year

9. Say the part of each name above that tells about length.

10. a. Which arrow shows the way the air will leave the balloon?

    b. Which arrow shows the way the balloon will move?

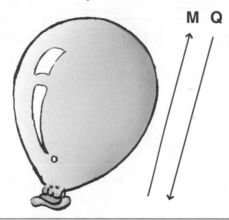

11. The drops of water you can see on grass early in the morning are called ▇▇▇.

12. If a grain of sugar were very big, it would look like a box made of ▇▇▇.

2. Say the letter of every hair that is being pushed down.

3. Say the letter of every hair that is being pulled up.

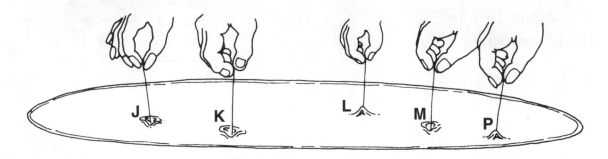

4. When we weigh very small things, the unit we use is ████ .

5. a. How fast is truck A going?

   b. How fast is truck B going?

   c. Which truck is going faster?

6. How far is it from New York City to San Francisco?

7. Tell **how far** or **how fast** for each item.

   a. The bus went 50 miles.

   b. The bus went 50 miles per hour.

8. Tell the letter of the ruler that will make:

    a. the highest sound

    b. the lowest sound

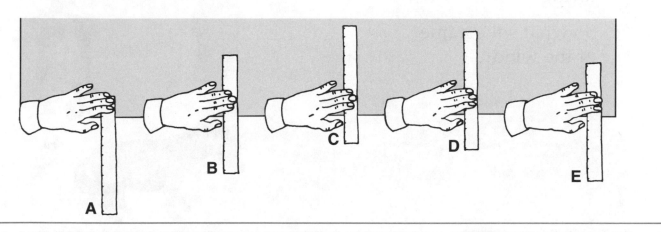

9. When we talk about miles per hour, we tell how ▬ something is moving.

10. When something tries to move in one direction, something else tries to move ▬.

11. Say the letters of the 3 animals that eat more every day than they weigh.

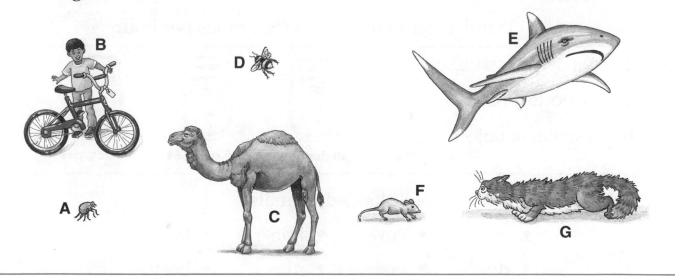

12. If you get smaller, your voice gets ▬.

2. a. Which animal is facing into the wind?

   b. Which direction is that animal facing?

   c. So what's the name of the wind?

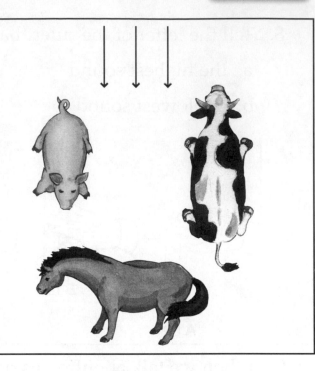

3. Tell how fast each object can go.

   a. a fast dog

   b. a jet

   c. a fast man

   - 20 miles per hour
   - 35 miles per hour
   - 200 miles per hour
   - 500 miles per hour

4. Tell the temperature of:

   a. the hottest object

   b. the coldest object

40 degrees   **80 degrees**   **60 degrees**

5. Say the names of the cold-blooded animals.

   - ant
   - cow
   - horse
   - flea
   - dog
   - bee
   - pig
   - beetle

6. As you touch places A and B, say the letter. Then tell the name of the place.

7. As you touch places C and D, say the letter. Then tell the name of the place.

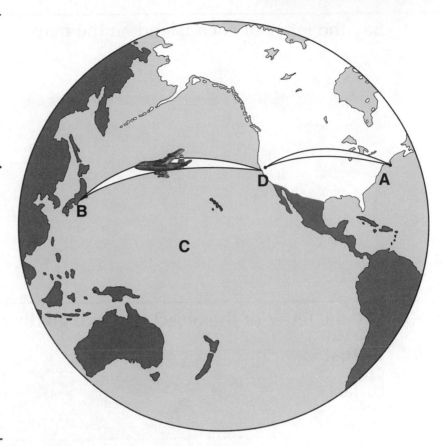

8. How far is it:

   a. from New York City to San Francisco?

   b. from San Francisco to Japan?

9. Answer these questions about the United States.

   a. How many states are there?

   b. What's the biggest state?

10. In which picture is the water

    a. getting hotter?

    b. getting colder?

11. What's the boiling temperature of water?

12. In San Francisco the wind blows from the to the .

2. Say the letter of each island on the map.

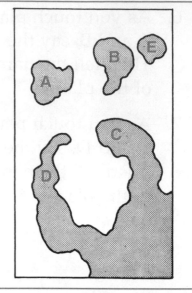

3. Say the letter of the object that will go down the whirlpool:

   a. first

   b. last

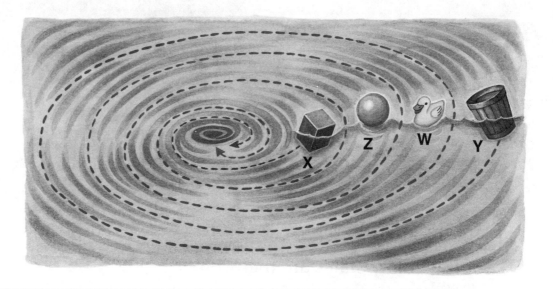

4. a. Which jar is heavier?

   b. Which jar will freeze at 32 degrees?

X
OCEAN WATER

Y
FRESH WATER

5. The arrow by the handle shows which way it turns. Say the letter of the arrow that shows the way:

   a. the log moves

   b. the vine moves

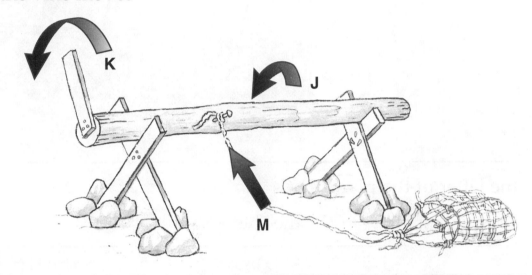

6. As you touch places A and B, say the letter. Then tell the name of the place.

7. As you touch places C and D, say the letter. Then tell the name of the place.

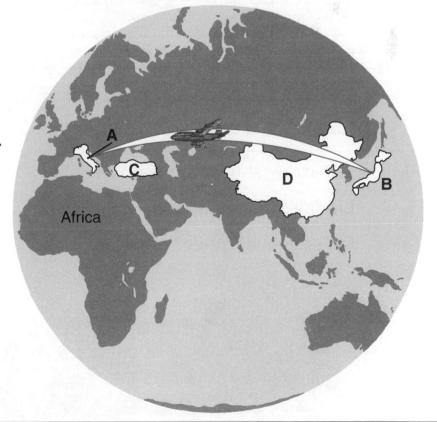

8. Say the letter of the handle that would give you:

   a. the most power

   b. the least power

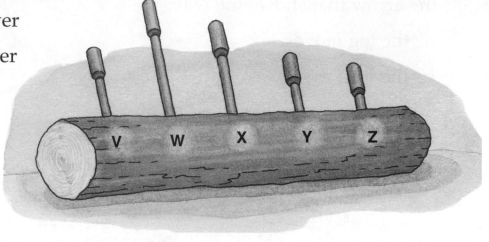

9. Say the letter of the plane that's in:

   a. the warmest air   b. the coldest air

	5 miles high
J	4 miles high
K	3 miles high
L	2 miles high
	1 mile high
M	

10. Which arrow shows the way:

    a. Linda's hand will move?

    b. the crate will move?

Q →

P ←

11. Tell the 3 places that are in the United States.

- Texas
- China
- Italy
- New York City
- Alaska
- Turkey

12. As you touch each letter, say the letter. Then name the part.

Fact Game

2. a. How many ships sailed to Troy?
   b. How long did the war between Troy and Greece go on?
   c. Who won the war?
3. Answer these questions about the war between Troy and Greece.
   a. What did the Greek army build?
   b. What was inside the object?
   c. What did they do after they came out of the object?
4. a. Airplanes are pulled by little trucks. Ships are pulled by ____.
   b. Airplanes unload at gates. Ships unload at ____.
   c. Airplanes land at airports. Ships land at ____.
5. a. When you're healthy, your body temperature is about ____ degrees.
   b. Most fevers don't go over ____ degrees.
6. Tell when
   a. the first airplane was made
   b. the United States became a country
   c. Troy went to war
7. Tell the year
   a. now
   b. 1 hundred years ago
   c. 2 hundred years ago
8. Tell the year
   a. now
   b. 3 hundred years ago

9. As you touch places A, B, and C, say the letter. Then tell the name of the place.

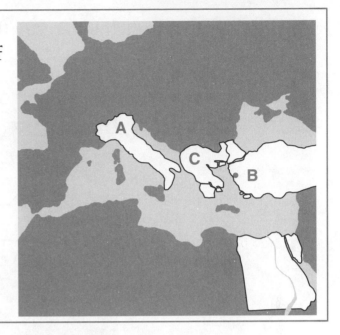

10. Tell the letter of the sun you see:

a. at noon

b. early in the morning

c. at sunset

11. a. Greece went to war with Troy because of a woman named ▮▮▮.

b. That woman was important because she was a ▮▮▮.

c. She went away with a man from ▮▮▮.

12. The place that is called Troy is now part of the country of ▮▮▮.

2. As you touch each letter, say the letter. Then tell the name of the place.

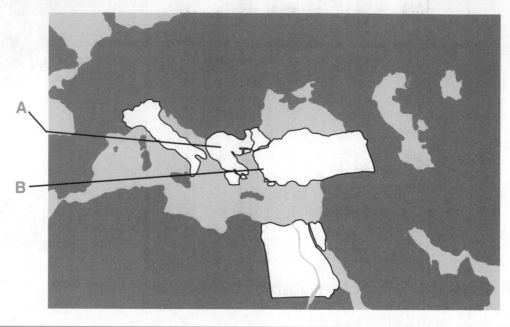

3. a. How long was Troy at war with Greece?

   b. What did the Greek army build?

   c. Who won?

4. Gasoline comes from a liquid called ▬▬.

5. As you touch each letter, say the letter. Then tell if it shows the **crude oil,** the **pipeline,** or the **refinery.**

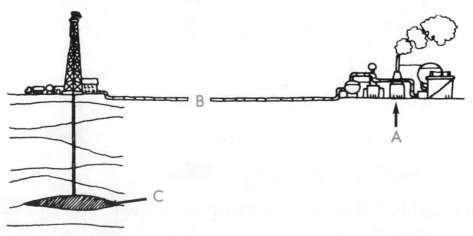

6. Which arrow shows the direction the crude oil is moving:

   a. at A?

   b. at B?

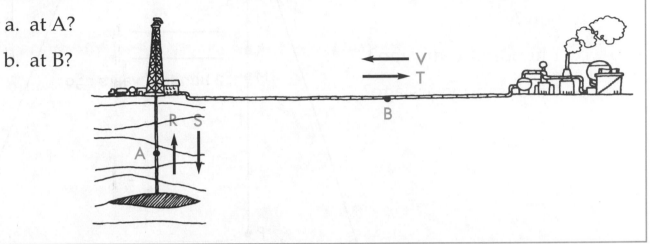

7. As you touch each letter, say the letter. Then tell if it shows **crude oil, salt water,** or **fresh water.**

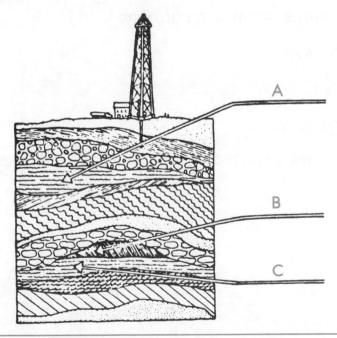

8. Say the sentence using other words for **weakness:** His love of candy was his **weakness.**

9. Name 2 kinds of wells.

10. Which letter shows:

    a. now?

    b. 1 hundred years ago?

    c. 1 thousand years ago?

    J •
    K •
    M • **2 hundred years ago**

    P •

11. Tell when

    a. the United States became a country.

    b. Troy went to war.

12. Tell the year

    a. 1 hundred years ago.

    b. 2 hundred years ago.

2. a. Which army was Achilles in during the war between Troy and Greece?

   b. How long was he in the war?

   c. Who won when he fought against Hector?

3. a. Who was the greatest soldier of Troy?

   b. Achilles rode around the wall of Troy in a ▮▮.

4. a. Name a good place to look for clues about people who lived long ago.

   b. Tell when eohippus lived.

---

5. As you touch each horse, say the letter. Then name the horse.

 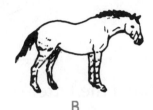 

A   B   C

---

6. a. Things closer to the top of the pile went into the pile ▮▮.

   b. Things closer to the bottom of the pile went into the pile ▮▮.

Fact Game

7. Which thing went into this pile **earlier?**

   a. W or B

   b. F or H

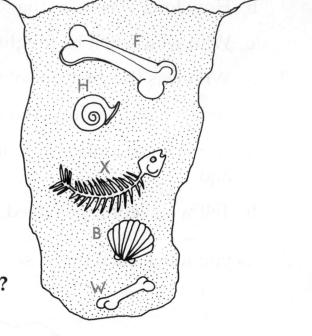

8. Which thing went into this pile **later?**

   a. W or X

   b. H or B

9. When we dig into the pile, what's the letter of

   a. the first thing we find?

   b. the next thing we find?

   c. the last thing we find?

10. Tell how many third-graders weigh as much as a

    a. draft horse

    b. racehorse

    c. Mongolian horse

11. a. 80 thousand years ago, some people lived in ▮▮▮ instead of houses.

    b. How does fire like to move, up or down?

12. Which comes first—lightning or thunder?

2. a. Electricity can turn a steel bar into an ▬.

   b. Name a place where these magnets are used.

3. a. How long is a football field?

   b. Tell 2 ways that a football team can move the ball down the field.

4. A second is a unit of ▬. • length • weight • time • distance

5. a. About how much does a leopard weigh?

   b. About how much weight can a leopard carry?

   • 150 pounds • 500 pounds • 100 pounds

6. a. About how much does a chimpanzee weigh?

   b. About how much force can a chimpanzee pull with?

7. As you touch **A** and **B,** say the letter. Then tell how much time has passed on the stopwatch.

8. a. When was this check written?

   b. Who should the bank pay?

   May 20, 1998

   Pay to ___Ted Rose___ , $15

   ___Fifteen___ ──────── dollars

   Rod Mack

9. a. How much should the bank pay?

   b. Whose money should the bank use?

10. Tell the letter of:

   a. the shortest hang-time

   b. the longest hang-time

A – 6 seconds	C – 2 seconds
B – 4 seconds	D – 3 seconds

11. As you touch **A** and **B,** say the letter. Then name the part of the uniform.

A

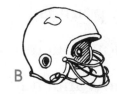
B

12. If the hang-time for a kick is 6 seconds, how long does the ball stay in the air?

Fact Game

2. As you touch each horse, say the letter. Then name the horse.

 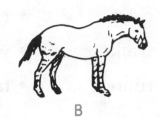 

A   B   C

3. a. Things closer to the bottom of the pile went into the pile ▆▆▆.

   b. Things closer to the top of the pile went into the pile ▆▆▆.

4. When we dig into the pile, what's the letter of

   a. the first thing we find?

   b. the next thing we find?

   c. the last thing we find?

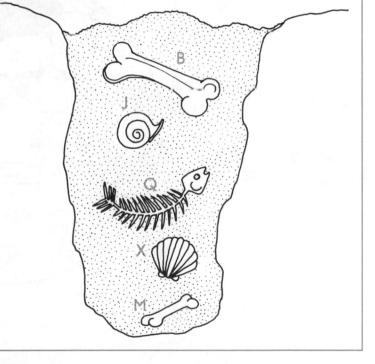

5. Read all the relatives of the word **hop.**

      • hopped   • mopping   • hotter

      • shot   • hopper   • hopping

6. Read all the words in the **walk** family.

    - jump
    - book
    - eats
    - walker

    - running
    - rider
    - walks
    - runner

    - sat
    - ran
    - walked
    - talking

7. Read all the words in the **run** family.

8. As you touch each letter, say the letter. Then tell the name of the place.

9. As you touch each letter, say the letter. Then tell the name of the place.

10. What happened in place **M** about 3 thousand years ago?

11. Tell the year

    a. the United States became a country.

    b. the first airplane was made.

12. Tell the year

    a. 1 hundred years ago.

    b. 2 hundred years ago.

2. Answer these questions about a kangaroo:

   a. How far can it go in one jump?

   b. How long is it when it's born?

3. a. Where does a baby kangaroo live right after it's born?

   b. How long does it live there?

4. Tell which country:

   a. is just north of the United States

   b. has wild kangaroos

   c. has wild peacocks

5. If you go east from Australia, what ocean do you go through?

6. As you touch A and B, say the letter. Then tell the name of the place.

7. As you touch C, D and E, say the letter. Then tell the name of the place.

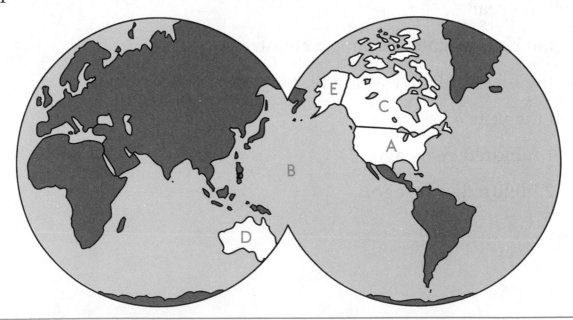

8. How many seconds are in one minute?

9. Answer these questions about Canada and the United States:

   a. Which country is **smaller?**

   b. Which country is **colder?**

   c. Where do **more** people live?

10. The hand on the clock that moves fast went around 5 times. How much time passed?

11. a. What's a group of kangaroos called?

    b. What's a baby kangaroo called?

12. As you touch each letter, say the letter. Then tell the name of the animal.

2. What do we call the mittens that boxers wear when they box?

3. A word that sounds the same as another word is called a ▨.

4. Which picture shows:

   a. the largest force?

   b. the smallest force?

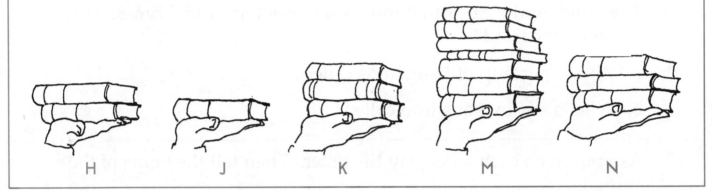

5. a. Which city had a great fire that burned down most of the city?

   b. In what year was that fire?

6. Tell the two words that make up:

   a. can't

   b. you've

   c. we're

7. For each word in the box, read the word. Then tell the letter of the word's homonym.

right	A – for
here	B – road
rode	C – write
four	D – hear

8. a. In a large city, what kind of buildings may be made of wood?

    • houses   • stores   • barns   • office buildings

    b. What kind of buildings are not made of wood?

9. Tell what year:

    a. Eric and Tom found the time machine.

    b. Thrig was from.

10. a. A force is a ▇▇▇.

    b. The greater the force, the harder the ▇▇▇.

11. Someone in Hohoboho said, "He has a **tear** on his cheek." The word that got the point rhymes with ▇▇▇.

    • here   • hair

12. What do you do to:

    a. close the door of the time machine?

    b. make the time machine move in time?

2. Tell the 3 years that are in the past.

3. Tell the 3 years that are in the future.

- 1868
- 2100
- 1796
- 2010
- 1996
- 2222

4. Say the 3 names that tell about distance or length.

5. Say the 3 names that tell about time.

6. Say the 3 names that tell about speed.

- inches per minute
- yards
- days
- hours
- meters per week
- feet
- feet per second
- centimeters
- weeks

10. As you touch countries A, B, and C, say the letter. Then tell the name of the country.

11. As you touch countries D and E, say the letter. Then tell the name of the country.

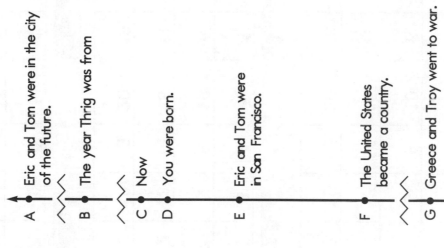

AFRICA

12. Tell the 3 places that are in the United States.
 • Texas   • Canada
 • Greece   • New York City
 • Spain   • Concord

7. As you touch dots A, B, and C, say the letter. Then read the event and tell what time each event tells about.

A • Eric and Tom were in the city of the future.

B • The year Thrig was from

C • Now
D • You were born.

E • Eric and Tom were in San Francisco.

F • The United States became a country.

G • Greece and Troy went to war.

H • Eric and Tom were in Egypt.

I • Eric and Tom saw a saber-toothed tiger.

8. As you touch dots D, E, and F, say the letter. Then tell what time each event tells about.

9. As you touch dots G, H, and I, say the letter. Then tell what time each event tells about.

Fact Game Scorecards

Lesson 30

1	2	3	4	5
6	7	8	9	10
11	12	13	14	15
16	17	18	19	20

Lesson 40

1	2	3	4	5
6	7	8	9	10
11	12	13	14	15
16	17	18	19	20

Lesson 50

1	2	3	4	5
6	7	8	9	10
11	12	13	14	15
16	17	18	19	20

Lesson 60

1	2	3	4	5
6	7	8	9	10
11	12	13	14	15
16	17	18	19	20

Lesson 70

1	2	3	4	5
6	7	8	9	10
11	12	13	14	15
16	17	18	19	20

Lesson 80

1	2	3	4	5
6	7	8	9	10
11	12	13	14	15
16	17	18	19	20

Lesson 90

1	2	3	4	5
6	7	8	9	10
11	12	13	14	15
16	17	18	19	20

Lesson 100

1	2	3	4	5
6	7	8	9	10
11	12	13	14	15
16	17	18	19	20

Lesson 110

1	2	3	4	5
6	7	8	9	10
11	12	13	14	15
16	17	18	19	20

Lesson 120

1	2	3	4	5
6	7	8	9	10
11	12	13	14	15
16	17	18	19	20

Lesson 130

1	2	3	4	5
6	7	8	9	10
11	12	13	14	15
16	17	18	19	20

Lesson 140

1	2	3	4	5
6	7	8	9	10
11	12	13	14	15
16	17	18	19	20

APPENDIX H — GROUP SUMMARY CHART

Teacher _____   Reading Mastery Plus Level 3   Group_____

Lessons	__1	__2	__3	__4	CO __5	__6	__7	__8	__9	CO/Test __	
Main Story Errors											
Name	IW	IW	IW	IW	CO	IW	IW	IW	IW	IW	CO	Test

Reading Mastery Plus Level 3

Reading Checkout lessons

Teacher __Ms. Turner__

Group __2__

Independent Work

Lessons	4 1	4 2	4 3	4 4	CO 4 5	4 6	4 7	4 8	4 9	CO/Test 5	
Main Story Errors	7	8	8	8	(9)	11	7	5	9		
Name	IW	IW	IW	IW	CO	IW	IW	IW	IW	IW	CO	Test
Luis Cepeda	2	1	2	1	P/0	2	1	0	1	3	P/0	2
Yoko Higashi	(4)	3	2	2	P/0	2	3	1	2	2	P/1	2
Anita Diaz	1	1	1	0	P/0	2	1	1	0	2	P/0	0
Denise Barton	1	2	0	1	(F)/1	1	0	1	0	2	P/2	(5)
Zachary Gray	1	0	0	1	P/0	1	2	1	1	1	P/0	0
Eric Adler	2	1	1	0	P/1	1	0	1	0	2	P/1	2

For all categories, circle any non-passing mark.

Main Story Errors Record number of errors group makes during main-story reading.

Independent Work (IW) Record number of errors. Passing criterion: 3 or fewer errors.

Reading Checkouts (CO) Record number of errors in lower part of box. Record P or F in upper part of box. Passing (P) is 100 (or more) wpm with 2 or fewer errors.

Test Record number of errors. See Test Summary Sheet (Appendix I) for passing criteria.

For more details, see pages 43, 58, 61, and 68 of this guide.

APPENDIX I—TEST SUMMARY SHEET

Name	Test 1	Test 2	Test 3	Test 4	Test 5	Test 6	Test 7	Test 8
Passing Criterion	22/24	20/22	22/25	23/26	30/33	29/32	32/36	26/29

APPENDIX I—TEST SUMMARY SHEET

Name	Test 9	Test 10	Test 11	Test 12	Test 13	Test 14	End-of-Program Test
Passing Criterion	32/36	24/27	16/18	29/32	30/33	32/36	27/30

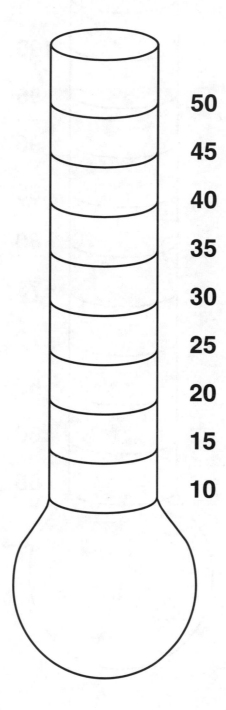

50

45

40

35

30

25

20

15

10

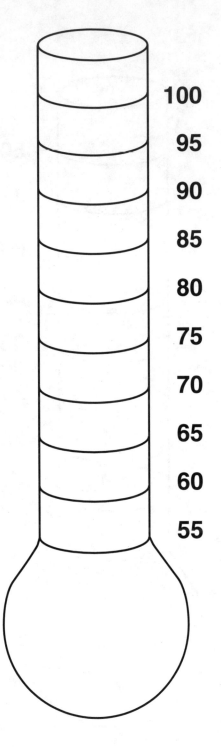

100

95

90

85

80

75

70

65

60

55

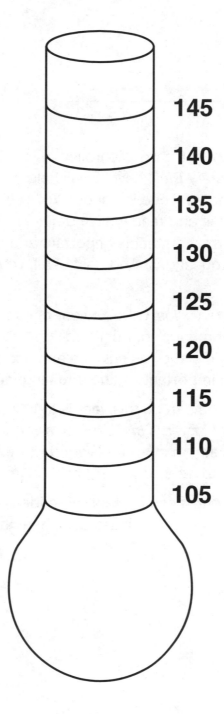

145

140

135

130

125

120

115

110

105

Level 3, Letter 1

To the family of _____

     This school year your child is enrolled in the *Reading Mastery Plus* program. *Reading Mastery Plus,* Level 3 will help your child learn the reading skills needed to succeed in school. Your child will learn how to sound out difficult words and read well and quickly. Your child will learn how to remember information that is important and how to use that information to answer questions. And best of all, your child will find that reading is enjoyable.

     In *Reading Mastery Plus,* Level 3, your child will develop the ability to "read to learn." That means your child will be able to read with better understanding in subjects such as science and social studies. In addition, your child will work on important writing and language arts skills.

     The best thing you can do this year is to let your child know that the work done in *Reading Mastery Plus,* Level 3 is very important. Encourage your child to read something at home every day. Remind your child "the more you read, the better reader you will be."

     If you have any questions or want more ideas about how to help your child with reading this year, please call me at the school. I'll be happy to talk with you.

Thank you,

_____

Para la familia de _____

      Este año escolar su hijo está inscrito en el programa de *Reading Mastery Plus. Reading Mastery Plus,* Level 3 ayudará a su hijo a aprender las destrezas de lectura necesarias para triunfar en la escuela. Su hijo aprenderá a pronunciar palabras dificiles y a leer mejor y rápidamente. Aprenderá a recordar información que es importante y cómo usarla para responder preguntas. Y lo mejor de todo es que su hijo descubrirá que leer es divertido.

      En *Reading Mastery Plus,* Level 3, su hijo desarrollará la capacidad de "leer para aprender". Eso significa que su hijo será capaz de leer entendiendo mejor materias como ciencias y estudios sociales. Además trabajará en destrezas de escritura y artes del lenguaje importantes.

      Lo mejor que usted pude hacer este año es dejar que su hijo sepa que el trabajo que hace en *Reading Mastery Plus,* Level 3, es muy importante. Anímelo a leer algo en la casa diariamente. Recuérdele a su hijo que "mientras más lea, un mejor lector será".

      Si tiene alguna pregunta o quiere más ideas acerca de cómo ayudar a su hijo con la lectura este año, por favor llámeme a la escuela. Me encantará hablar con usted.

Gracias,

_____

To the family of _____

 Your child has completed _____ lessons of *Reading Mastery Plus,* Level 3. Every day your child has worked on skills needed to read better and faster. During this school term, your child has learned how to read hundreds of new words. Every day, your child has read information articles and stories. Your child has learned how to remember and use the information read in the articles and stories. These are important skills that will lead to success next year in school and in all the years to come.

 During this break in the school year, encourage your child to read something every day. As in anything we attempt to learn, reading takes practice and lots of it. Remind your child "the more you read, the better reader you will be." Tell your child you are proud of the progress he or she is making.

 If you have any questions or want more ideas about how to help your child with reading during this break in the school year, please call me at the school. I'll be happy to talk with you.

Thank you,

_____

Para la familia de _____

Su hijo ha terminado _____ lecciones de *Reading Mastery Plus,*
Level 3. Cada día su hijo ha trabajado en las destrezas necesarias para
leer mejor y más rápido. Durante este período escolar su hijo ha
aprendido a cómo leer cientos de palabras nuevas. Su hijo ha leído
artículos informativos e historias diariamente. Ha aprendido a cómo
recordar y usar la información que leyó en los artículos e historias. Éstas
son destrezas importantes que conducirán al éxito en el próximo año
escolar y en los años venideros.

Durante este receso del año escolar, anime a su hijo a leer algo
diariamente. La lectura requiere mucha práctica al igual que todo lo que
intentamos aprender. Recuérdele a su hijo que "mientras más lea, un
mejor lector será". Dígale que usted está orgulloso de su progreso.

Si usted tiene preguntas o quiere más ideas acerca de cómo
ayudar a su hijo con la lectura durante este receso del año escolar, por
favor llámeme a la escuela. Me encantará hablar con usted.

Gracias,

_____

APPENDIX L—SAMPLE LESSON

71

A

1
1. Mr. Daniels
2. recognize
3. elevator
4. medicine
5. guess
6. dozen

2
1. silently
2. watering
3. heater
4. approached
5. fairly

3
1. clues
2. doctors
3. offices
4. drugs
5. typists
6. lawyers

4
1. cock your head
2. equipment
3. motorcycle
4. refinery
5. friendly
6. unfriendly

5
1. explain
2. insist
3. honest
4. crude
5. fifth

6
1. narrow
2. prison
3. polite
4. several
5. pipeline

B **Oil Wells**

A well is a deep hole in the ground. The well has pipe in it so the hole stays open.

There are different types of wells.

- Some wells are fresh-water wells. These wells pump fresh water from under the ground.

• Some wells are oil wells. These wells pump crude oil from under the ground.

Picture 1 shows a machine that is drilling a hole for a well.

If the machine keeps drilling, what type of liquid will it reach first?

If the machine keeps drilling past the fresh water, what kind of liquid will it reach next?

If the machine keeps drilling, what will it reach after the oil?

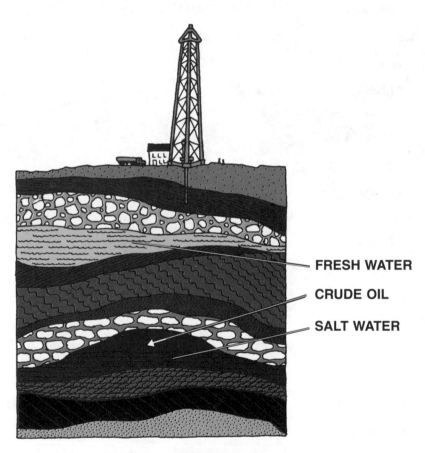

FRESH WATER

CRUDE OIL

SALT WATER

PICTURE 1

If the well is an oil well, it pumps crude oil from the ground. Crude oil is a dark liquid that can be changed to make things like gasoline, motor oil, and plastic.

The crude oil is pumped from the well. Then it goes into a pipeline. The pipeline goes along the ground and carries the crude oil many miles to a refinery.

The refinery is a large place with strange-looking equipment and large tanks for holding oil.

The refinery changes crude oil into gasoline and other things.

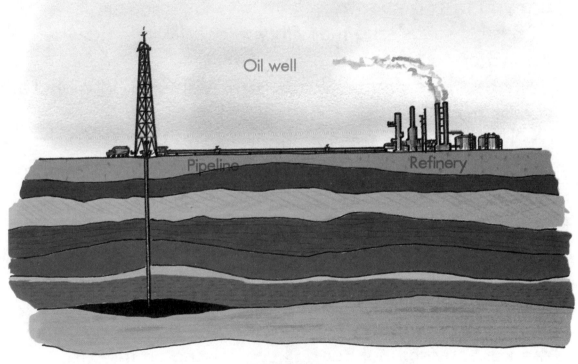

PICTURE 2

C Maria Tests Bertha's Talent

Bertha had a plan for helping Maria figure out where the water came from. You probably know what her plan was. Although Bertha didn't know too much about oil wells and refineries, she did know that she could smell the difference between water taken from the creek and water taken from water wells.

Bertha was sitting on Maria's porch. She said, "Maria, it's easy for me to tell if the water comes from the creek or from the well. I'll just smell it."

Maria looked slowly at Bertha and made a face. "What are you talking about?"

Bertha said, "Take me with you and I'll tell you where the water comes from."

Maria made another face. "How will you know where it comes from?"

"I told you. I'll smell it," Bertha said. Then she explained her talent. "I can tell about anything by smelling it. Honest I can."

Maria cocked her head and looked at Bertha. "What is this, a joke?" Maria asked.

Bertha said, "Give me a test. Get glasses of water from different places. I'll tell you where you got each glass of water." At first Maria didn't want to do it. "This is crazy," she kept saying. But Bertha kept insisting on the test. Finally Maria went into her house and came back with three glasses of water. She said, "You ⭐ can't feel them, or you may get some clues about where I got them."

Bertha said, "I don't have to feel them. The one on the left is from your water heater. The middle glass is from a watering can or something like that. That water has been sitting out for a couple of days. The water in the last glass came from a water jug or something in your refrigerator. It's been in the refrigerator for a long time, and it probably doesn't taste very good."

"I don't believe this," Maria said, and she tasted the water from the last glass. She made a face. "Oh, you're right. It's bad."

Suddenly Maria laughed, turned around, and looked at Bertha. She said, "I don't believe this." Then she said, "I don't believe this," three or four more times. "You're amazing. You are amazing. You are the most amazing person I have ever seen."

She kept talking very fast. She told about some of the amazing things that she had seen—a cow with two heads and a building over 3 hundred meters high. Finally, she said, "I once saw a man jump a motorcycle over twenty cars and that was amazing, but you are five times as amazing."

"Can I go with you?" Bertha asked.

"Yes, yes, yes, yes, yes," Maria said. "This will be great."

MORE NEXT TIME

D Number your paper from 1 through 19.

Skill Items

> **Lawyers with talent normally succeed.**
> 1. What word means the opposite of **fail**?
> 2. What word names people who help us when we have questions about the law?
> 3. What word means **usually**?
> 4. What word refers to the special skills a person has?

Review Items

5. You can see drops of water on grass early in the morning. What are those called?

6. Which letter shows the coconut milk?
7. Which letter shows the inner shell?
8. Which letter shows the coconut meat?
9. Which letter shows the outer shell?

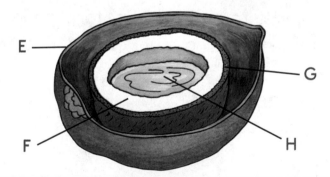

10. All machines make it easier for someone to ███.

11. You would have the most power if you pushed against one of the handles. Which handle is that?
12. Which handle would give you the least amount of power?

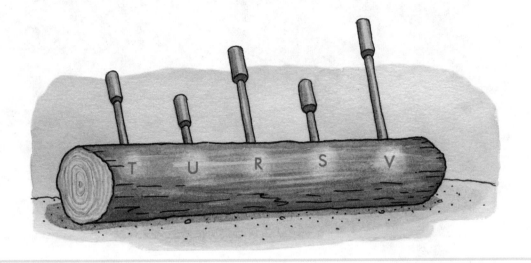

13. When people have very high fevers, how do they feel?
14. They may see and hear things that are not ███.

15. Write the letter that shows a tugboat.
16. Write two letters that show ships.
17. Write two letters that show docks.

18. The place that is called Troy is now part of what country?

  • Greece   • Italy   • Turkey

19. Write the letters of the 4 kinds of weapons that soldiers used when they had battles with Troy.

a. bows   c. arrows   e. spears   g. planes
b. swords   d. rockets   f. guns   h. tanks

Name _____

A

1. Name two kinds of wells. _____

Write these names on the picture to show where each liquid is: **crude oil, fresh water, salt water.**

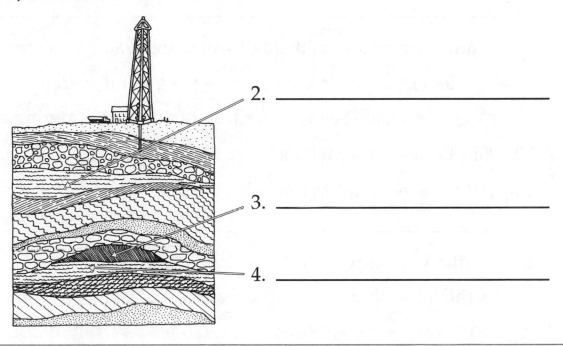

2. _____

3. _____

4. _____

5. Fill in the boxes with the names for the **crude oil, pipeline,** and **refinery.**

6. Draw an arrow at A to show which way the crude oil is moving.

7. Draw an arrow at B to show which way the crude oil is moving.

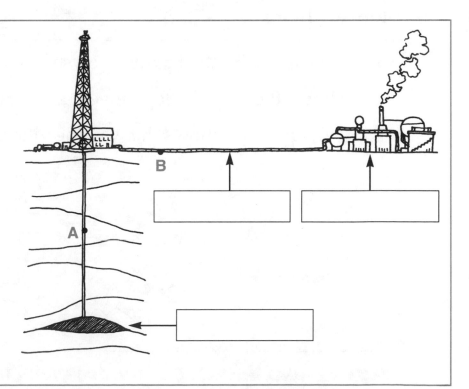

B Story Items

8. Gasoline comes from a liquid called _____.

9. When Bertha first told Maria about her talent, did Maria believe her?

   _____

10. How many glasses of water did Maria use to test Bertha's talent?

    _____

11. **Underline** the items that tell where the water came from.

    • fish bowl   • bath tub   • jug in refrigerator   • sink

    • water heater   • frog pond   • watering can

12. Did Bertha pass Maria's test? _____

13. After the test, did Maria believe what Bertha said about her talent?

    _____

14. Bertha will help Maria by telling where ▆▆▆.

    • the oil wells are   • the water came from   • the snow was

---

Review Items

15. The arrow by the handle shows which way it turns. Which arrow
    shows the way the log moves? _____

16. Which arrow shows the way the vine moves? _____

GO TO PART D IN YOUR TEXTBook.

Lesson 71

EXERCISE 1

VOCABULARY REVIEW

a. You learned a sentence that tells how long she survived.
- Everybody, say that sentence. Get ready. (Signal.) *She survived until she was rescued.*
- (Repeat until firm.)

b. You learned a sentence that tells what the soldiers did.
- Say that sentence. Get ready. (Signal.) *The soldiers protected their equipment.*
- (Repeat until firm.)

c. Here's the last sentence you learned: Lawyers with talent normally succeed.
- Everybody, say that sentence. Get ready. (Signal.) *Lawyers with talent normally succeed.*
- (Repeat until firm.)

d. Everybody, what do we call people who help us when we have questions about the law? (Signal.) *Lawyers.*
- What's another word for **usually**? (Signal.) *Normally.*
- What word refers to the special skills a person has? (Signal.) *Talent.*
- What word means the opposite of **fail**? (Signal.) *Succeed.*

e. Once more. Say the sentence that tells about lawyers with talent. Get ready. (Signal.) *Lawyers with talent normally succeed.*

EXERCISE 2

READING WORDS

Column 1

a. **Find lesson 71 in your textbook.** ✓
- Touch column 1. ✓
- (Teacher reference:)

1. **Mr. Daniels**	4. **medicine**
2. **recognize**	5. **guess**
3. **elevator**	6. **dozen**

b. Number 1 is the name **Mr. Daniels.** What name? (Signal.) *Mr. Daniels.*

c. Word 2 is **recognize.** What word? (Signal.) *Recognize.*

- When you **recognize** something that you see or feel, you know what it is. Here's another way of saying **She knew what the smell was: She recognized the smell.**

d. Your turn. What's another way of saying **She knew what the smell was?** (Signal.) *She recognized the smell.*
- (Repeat step d until firm.)

e. What's another way of saying **She knew who the person was?** (Signal.) *She recognized the person.*

f. Word 3 is **elevator.** What word? (Signal.) *Elevator.*
- Spell **elevator.** Get ready. (Tap for each letter.) *E-L-E-V-A-T-O-R.*

g. Word 4 is **medicine.** What word? (Signal.) *Medicine.*
- Spell **medicine.** Get ready. (Tap for each letter.) *M-E-D-I-C-I-N-E.*

h. Word 5 is **guess.** What word? (Signal.) *Guess.*
- Spell **guess.** Get ready. (Tap for each letter.) *G-U-E-S-S.*

i. Word 6 is **dozen.** What word? (Signal.) *Dozen.*
- Spell **dozen.** Get ready. (Tap for each letter.) *D-O-Z-E-N.*

j. Let's read those words again, the fast way.
- Number 1. What words? (Signal.) *Mr. Daniels.*

k. Word 2. What word? (Signal.) *Recognize.*
- (Repeat for words 3–6.)

l. (Repeat steps j and k until firm.)

Column 2

m. Find column 2. ✓
- (Teacher reference:)

1. **silently**	4. **approached**
2. **watering**	5. **fairly**
3. **heater**	

- All these words have endings.

n. Word 1. What word? (Signal.) *Silently.*
- (Repeat for words 2–5.)

o. (Repeat step n until firm.)

Column 3

p. Find column 3. ✓
- (Teacher reference:)

1. clues	4. drugs
2. doctors	5. typists
3. offices	6. lawyers

- All these words end with the letter **S**.

q. Word 1. What word? (Signal.) *Clues.*
- (Repeat for words 2–6.)

r. (Repeat step q until firm.)

Column 4

s. Find column 4. ✓
- (Teacher reference:)

1. cock your head	4. refinery
2. equipment	5. friendly
3. motorcycle	6. unfriendly

t. Number 1. What words? (Signal.) *Cock your head.*
- When you cock your head, you tilt it. Everybody, show me how you cock your head. ✓

u. Word 2. What word? (Signal.) *Equipment.*
- (Repeat for words 3–6.)

v. Let's read those words again.
- Number 1. What words? (Signal.) *Cock your head.*

w. Word 2. What word? (Signal.) *Equipment.*
- (Repeat for words 3–6.)

x. (Repeat steps v and w until firm.)

Column 5

y. Find column 5. ✓
- (Teacher reference:)

1. explain	4. crude
2. insist	5. fifth
3. honest	

z. Word 1. What word? (Signal.) *Explain.*
- When you **explain** something, you **tell about it.** Here's another way of saying **She told about her talent: She explained her talent.**

a. Your turn. What's another way of saying **She told about her talent?** (Signal.) *She explained her talent.*
- (Repeat step a until firm.)

b. What's another way of saying **He told about his plan?** (Signal.) *He explained his plan.*

c. Word 2. What word? (Signal.) *Insist.*
- (Repeat for words 3–5.)

d. Let's read those words again.
- Word 1. What word? (Signal.) *Explain.*
- (Repeat for words 2–5.)

e. (Repeat step d until firm.)

Column 6

f. Find column 6. ✓
- (Teacher reference:)

1. narrow	4. several
2. prison	5. pipeline
3. polite	

g. Word 1. What word? (Signal.) *Narrow.*
- (Repeat for words 2–5.)

h. (Repeat step g until firm.)

Individual Turns

(For columns 1–6: Call on individual students, each to read one to three words per turn.)

EXERCISE 3
COMPREHENSION PASSAGE

a. Find part B in your textbook. ✓
- You're going to read the next story about Bertha. First you'll read the information passage. It gives some facts about wells.

b. Everybody, touch the title. ✓
- (Call on a student to read the title.) *[Oil Wells.]*
- Everybody, what's the title? (Signal.) *Oil Wells.*

c. (Call on individual students to read the passage, each student reading two or three sentences at a time. Ask the specified questions as the students read.)

Oil Wells

A well is a deep hole in the ground. The well has pipe in it so the hole stays open.

- Why does the well have a pipe in it? (Call on a student. Idea: *So the hole stays open.*)

There are different types of wells.
• Some wells are fresh-water wells. These wells pump fresh water from under the ground.

• What do fresh-water wells do? (Call on a student. Idea: *Pump fresh water from under the ground.*)

• Some wells are oil wells. These wells pump crude oil from under the ground.

• What do oil wells do? (Call on a student. Idea: *Pump crude oil from under the ground.*)

Picture 1 shows a machine that is drilling a hole for a well.

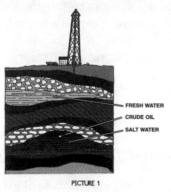

FRESH WATER
CRUDE OIL
SALT WATER

PICTURE 1

• Everybody, touch the underground pipe in picture 1 and show how far down the well is already dug. ✓

If the machine keeps drilling, what type of liquid will it reach first?

• Everybody, touch the liquid it will reach first. ✓
• What kind of liquid is that? (Signal.) *Fresh water.*

If the machine keeps drilling past the fresh water, what kind of liquid will it reach next?

• Everybody, touch the liquid it will reach next. ✓
• What kind of liquid is that? (Signal.) *Crude oil.*

If the machine keeps drilling, what will it reach after the oil?

• Everybody, touch the liquid it will reach next. ✓
• What kind of liquid is that? (Signal.) *Salt water.*
• If you dig a well deep enough, you'll always hit salt water.

If the well is an oil well, it pumps crude oil from the ground. Crude oil is a dark liquid that can be changed to make things like gasoline, motor oil, and plastic.

• What can be made from crude oil? (Call on a student.) *Gasoline, motor oil, plastic.*

The crude oil is pumped from the well. Then it goes into a pipeline.

• Everybody, where does the crude oil go from the well? (Signal.) *Into a pipeline.*

The pipeline goes along the ground and carries the crude oil many miles to a refinery.

• Everybody, where does the pipeline take the crude oil? (Signal.) *To a refinery.*
• Is the refinery usually right next to the well? (Signal.) *No.*

The refinery is a large place with strange-looking equipment and large tanks for holding oil.
The refinery changes crude oil into gasoline and other things.

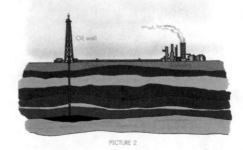

Oil well

PICTURE 2

• What does the refinery do? (Call on a student. Idea: *Changes crude oil into gasoline and other things.*)
• Everybody, touch the crude oil underground in picture 2. ✓
• Now follow it up the pipe to the surface of the ground. ✓
• Now follow it in the pipeline to the other end of the pipeline. ✓

- What's the other end? (Signal.) *The refinery.*
- What does that refinery do to the crude oil? (Call on a student. Idea: *Changes it into gasoline and other things.*)
- The oil company that you're reading about is a refinery.

EXERCISE 4

STORY READING

a. Find part C in your textbook. ✓
- The error limit for this story is 9. Read carefully.

b. Everybody, touch the title. ✓
- (Call on a student to read the title.) *[Maria Tests Bertha's Talent.]*
- What's going to happen in this story? (Call on a student. Idea: *Maria will test Bertha's talent.*)

c. (Call on individual students to read the story, each student reading two or three sentences at a time. Ask questions marked **1.**)

> - (Correct errors: Tell the word. Direct the student to reread the sentence.)
> - (If the group makes more than 9 errors, direct the students to reread the story.)

d. (After the group has read the selection making no more than 9 errors, read the story to the students and ask questions marked **2.**)

Maria Tests Bertha's Talent

Bertha had a plan for helping Maria figure out where the water came from. You probably know what her plan was.

1. What do you think it was? (Call on a student. Idea: *Get water from the oil company and have Bertha smell it to see whether it came from the creek or water wells.*)

Although Bertha didn't know too much about oil wells and refineries, she did know that she could smell the difference between water taken from the creek and water taken from water wells.

2. Everybody, where was the company supposed to be taking water from? (Signal.) *Wells.*

2. Where did Maria think it was coming from? (Signal.) *The creek.*

Bertha was sitting on Maria's porch. She said, "Maria, it's easy for me to tell if the water comes from the creek or from the well. I'll just smell it."

Maria looked slowly at Bertha and made a face. "What are you talking about?"

1. Everybody, show me the kind of face Maria probably made. ✓

1. What was Maria thinking about Bertha? (Call on a student. Idea: *That she was strange or crazy.*)

Bertha said, "Take me with you and I'll tell you where the water comes from."

Maria made another face. "How will you know where it comes from?"

"I told you. I'll smell it," Bertha said. Then she explained her talent.

1. How would she do that? (Call on a student. Idea: *By telling Maria how she used her sense of smell.*)

"I can tell about anything by smelling it. Honest I can."

Maria cocked her head and looked at Bertha.

2. Everybody, show me how you cock your head. ✓

"What is this, a joke?" Maria asked.

Bertha said, "Give me a test. Get glasses of water from different places. I'll tell you where you got each glass of water." At first Maria didn't want to do it. "This is crazy," she kept saying. But Bertha kept insisting on the test.

2. What would she say to keep insisting on the test? (Call on a student. Idea: *Get glasses of water from different places and I'll tell you where each one came from.*)

Finally Maria went into her house and came back with three glasses of water. She said, "You can't feel them, or you may get some clues about where I got them."

2. What kind of clues could you get by feeling the water glasses? (Call on a student. Idea: *Clues about temperature.*)

Bertha said, "I don't have to feel them. The one on the left is from your water heater.

2. What's a water heater? (Call on a student. Idea: *A machine that makes cold water get hot.*)

The middle glass is from a watering can or something like that.

2. What do you do with a watering can? (Call on a student. Idea: *Water plants and flowers.*)

That water has been sitting out for a couple of days. The water in the last glass came from a water jug or something in your refrigerator. It's been in the refrigerator for a long time, and it probably doesn't taste very good."
"I don't believe this," Maria said, and she tasted the water from the last glass. She made a face. "Oh, you're right. It's bad."

2. Everybody, show me the kind of face she made when she tasted the water. ✓

Suddenly Maria laughed, turned around, and looked at Bertha. She said, "I don't believe this." Then she said, "I don't believe this," three or four more times. "You're amazing. You are amazing. You are the most amazing person I have ever seen."
She kept talking very fast. She told about some of the amazing things that she had seen—a cow with two heads and a building over 3 hundred meters high. Finally, she said, "I once saw a man jump a motorcycle over twenty cars and that was amazing, but you are five times as amazing."

2. Maria is really excited. I'll read that part again. Listen to how she talks on and on.

Suddenly Maria laughed, turned around, and looked at Bertha. She said, "I don't believe this." Then she said, "I don't believe this," three or four more times. "You're amazing. You are amazing. You are the most amazing person I have ever seen."
She kept talking very fast. She told about some of the amazing things that she had seen—a cow with two heads and a building over 3 hundred meters high. Finally, she said, "I once saw a man jump a motorcycle over twenty cars and that was amazing, but you are five times as amazing."

"Can I go with you?" Bertha asked. "Yes, yes, yes, yes, yes," Maria said. "This will be great."
MORE NEXT TIME

1. Go back to the beginning of the story. Follow along while I read.
2. What do you think is going to happen? (Call on a student. Idea: *Maria will get Bertha to smell the water the oil company uses;* etc.)

EXERCISE 5
PAIRED PRACTICE

You're going to read aloud to your partner. Today the **B** members will read first. Then the **A** members will read from the star to the end of the story.
(Observe students and give feedback.)

End-of-Lesson Activities

INDEPENDENT WORK

Now finish your independent work for lesson 71. Raise your hand when you're finished.
(Observe students and give feedback.)

WORKCHECK

a. (Direct students to take out their marking pencils.)
• We're going to check your independent work. Remember, if you got an item wrong, make an **X** next to the item. Don't change any answers.

b. (For each item: Read the item. Call on a student to answer it. If the answer is wrong, say the correct answer. Refer to the Answer Key for the correct answers.)

c. Now use your marking pencil to fix up any items you got wrong. Remember, all mistakes must be fixed up before you hand in your independent work.

(Present Writing-Spelling lesson 71 after completing Reading lesson 71. See Writing-Spelling Guide.)

(Present Language Arts lesson 71 after completing Reading lesson 71. See Language Arts Guide.)

The *Reading Mastery Plus* program is based on the underlying concept that all children can learn if carefully taught. The program provides the kind of careful instruction that is needed to teach basic reading, literature, writing, and spelling skills.

The sequence of skills in *Reading Mastery Plus* Level 3 is controlled so that the student performs confidently the skills at each step before going on to more complicated tasks. The program builds on the skills developed in *Reading Mastery Plus* Level 2 and also teaches new concepts in the following areas:

Reading—sound combinations and words; reading vocabulary; story reading; story comprehension, literal and inferential; reasoning skills; literary skills; study skills; and following directions.

Literature—realistic fiction; fantasy; and non-fiction.

Writing and Spelling—word writing; sentence writing; word spelling; and spelling patterns.

Language Arts—reference material; grammar; alphabetical order; study skills; fact/opinion; listening skills; writing; technology; and vocabulary.

Activities Across the Curriculum—activities in science; social studies; math; writing; and art.

In addition, students have an opportunity to improve and expand independent work skills through workbook exercises. Picture and reading comprehension is taught as students complete exercises related to stories or factual passages previously read. Spelling skills are practiced as students use spelling words to complete workbook activities.

Scope and Sequence

The Scope and Sequence on page 174 provides a quick overview of *Reading Mastery Plus* Level 3. The Scope and Sequence lists the various tracks (skills) that are taught and the range of lessons for each track.

Behavioral Objectives

This information gives a comprehensive picture of *Reading Mastery Plus* Level 3. It focuses on the general curriculum goals of the program and on special behavioral goals to be achieved by individual students.

The Behavioral Objectives, which begin on page 175, cover the major skill areas, or tracks, within each of the areas of Reading; Literature; Writing and Spelling; and Activities Across the Curriculum shown on the Scope and Sequence. The chart is divided into four sections:

- The **Purpose of the track** is the general curriculum objective.

- The **Behavioral Objective** is the kind of performance that can be expected from the student who has mastered the skill.

- The section headed **The student is asked to** describes the specific kinds of tasks the student performs in order to master the skill.

- The section headed **First appears in** or **First appears after** shows where the skill is first introduced in the program.

Scope and Sequence

The following scope and sequence provides an overview of the skills taught in *Reading Mastery Plus,* Level 3. The skills are divided into eight principal areas: decoding, comprehension, literary skills, study skills, writing and spelling, literature, language arts, and activities across the curriculum.

DECODING

- Reading sound combinations: 1–145
- Reading words: 1–145
- Reading Vocabulary: 1–145
- Sentences and stories: 1–145
- Reading checkouts: 10–145, every fifth lesson

COMPREHENSION

- Comprehension readiness: 1–145
- Vocabulary: 4–145
- Literal comprehension: 1–145
- Interpretive comprehension: 1–145
- Reasoning skills: 1–145
- Content knowledge: 1–145

LITERARY SKILLS

- Analyzing characters and setting: 4–145
- Types of literature: 1–145
- Quotation marks: 8–145

STUDY SKILLS

- Writing answers to questions: 1–145
- Using reference material: 1–145

WRITING AND SPELLING

- Copy a sentence: 11–75
- Write main-idea sentences: 76–145
- Word spelling: 1–145
- Spelling patterns: 6–145

LITERATURE

- Reading Literature Lessons: 10–140, every tenth lesson, and lessons 6 and 115

LANGUAGE ARTS

- Reference Material: 51–140
- Grammar: 53–64
- Alphabetical Order: 61–103
- Study Skills: 65–73
- Fact vs. Opinion: 71
- Listening Skills: 72–88
- Writing: 73–88
- Technology: 81–88
- Vocabulary: 83–118

ACTIVITIES ACROSS THE CURRICULUM

- Participate in activities in science, social studies, math, writing, and art

Behavioral Objectives

Purpose of the track	Behavioral objectives	The student is asked to	First appears in lesson:
DECODING SKILLS: SOUNDS To teach the student to decode sounds	When presented with sound combinations, the student reads the sound combination correctly.	Read the following sound combinations correctly:	1
		ce	7
		ou	7
		ir	7
		oa	15
		ar	18
		al	18
		aw	18
		oi	23
		ee	25
		ea (long)	25
		mb	26
		ew	38
		ea (short)	115
DECODING SKILLS: WORDS To teach the student to decode words	When presented with a list of regularly spelled words, the student reads the words without error.	Read each word without error.	1
	When presented with a list of hard words, the student repeats the word, spells the word, then reads the word without error.	Repeat each word, spell each word, then read each word without error.	1
	When presented with a list of words with endings, the student reads each word without error.	Read words with the following endings:	
		s	1
		es	1
		ed	3
		ing	4
		y	17
		tion	18
		sion	18
		ly	29
		er	31

		n	37
		th	37
		's	37
		est	43
		ment	53
		or	69
		able	75
		ful	122
	When presented with irregularly spelled words, the student reads the list without error.	Read a list of irregularly spelled words.	1
	When presented with a list of words with underlined parts, the student reads the underlined part and then reads the whole word.	Read the underlined part and then read the whole word.	3
	When presented with a list of compound words, the student reads the first part, then reads the entire word.	Read parts of compound words and then read the entire word.	6
	When presented with a list of words, the student reads the list without error.	Orally read a list of words without making an error.	1
	When presented with a list of multi-syllable words, the student reads the first syllable, then reads the entire word.	Read syllables of a word then read the entire word.	3
	When presented with a list of words with the same beginning sound(s), the student reads the list without error.	Read words with the following beginning sound(s):	
		sw	55
		w	108
	When presented with a word that has homonyms or homographs, the student identifies them.	Write a homonym(s) for a given word.	123
		Identify the correct pronunciation of a homograph.	126
	When presented with a contraction, the student identifies the words that make up the contraction.	Write the two words that make up a given contraction.	127
DECODING SKILLS: SENTENCES AND STORIES To teach the student to read stories	When presented with a reading selection, the student reads it aloud with a minimum of decoding errors.	Read part of a textbook selection aloud.	1
		Read aloud in pairs.	6
	When presented with a reading selection, the student reads it silently.	Read part of a textbook selection silently.	92
READING CHECKOUTS To teach the student to read with increased speed and accuracy	When presented with a passage, the student reads it aloud within a specific time and decoding error limit.	Orally read a specified textbook passage in one minute or less with a minimum of decoding errors.	10–145 every fifth lesson

Teacher Presentation Book Lessons (continued)

COMPREHENSION SKILLS: READINESS To teach the student to follow directions	When given oral directions, the student follows them accurately.	Follow directions presented orally by the teacher.	1
	When presented with a picture, the student responds to tasks based on it.	Respond to tasks based on pictures in the textbook.	6
COMPREHENSION SKILLS: VOCABULARY To teach the student to understand and use vocabulary	When presented with the definition of a vocabulary word, the student comprehends the definition.	Explain the meaning of a defined vocabulary word.	4
	When presented with a vocabulary word, the student uses the word correctly in a sentence.	Use a vocabulary word correctly in a sentence.	4
	When presented with proper nouns, the student reads the words correctly.	Read proper nouns correctly.	11
	When presented with "time" words, the student reads the words correctly.	Read "time" words correctly.	12
	When presented with an underlined word or words, the student chooses another word that means the same thing.	Choose a word that means the same thing as an underlined word or words.	16
COMPREHENSION SKILLS: LITERAL COMPREHENSION To teach the student to focus on the literal meaning of a story or information when reading	When presented with facts and rules, the student memorizes them.	Memorize facts and rules presented in the textbook.	1
		Respond orally to facts and rules.	1
		Respond in writing to questions in the textbook about facts and rules.	1
		Complete workbook exercises by recalling facts and rules.	1
	When presented with literal questions about a reading selection, the student answers the questions.	Answer literal questions about a textbook selection.	1
		Respond in writing to literal questions in the textbook.	1
		Complete workbook exercises by answering literal questions.	1
	After reading a selection, the student recalls details and events from the selection.	Answer questions about a textbook selection by recalling details and events.	1
		Respond in writing to questions in the textbook about details and events.	1
		Complete workbook exercises by recalling details and events.	1
	After reading a selection, the student identifies literal causes and effects within the selection.	Answer questions about a textbook selection by identifying literal cause and effect.	1
		Complete workbook exercises by identifying literal causes and effects.	1
	When presented with written directions, the student follows them correctly.	Follow written directions.	1

COMPREHENSION SKILLS: INTERPRETIVE COMPREHENSION To teach the student to focus on the inferred meanings in a story or information when reading	While reading a story, the student predicts a possible story outcome.	Predict the outcome of a textbook story.	1
	When presented with a story title, the student predicts the content of the story.	Use a textbook story's title to predict its content.	1
	After reading a selection, the student infers causes and effects within the selection.	Answer questions about a textbook selection by inferring causes and effects.	1
		Respond in writing to inferential cause and effect questions in the textbook.	1
		Complete workbook exercises by inferring causes and effects.	1
	After reading a selection, the student infers details and events within the selection.	Answer questions about a textbook selection by inferring details and events.	1
		Respond in writing to inferential detail and event questions in the textbook.	1
		Complete workbook exercises by inferring details and events.	1
	When presented with a deduction, the student uses the deduction to complete workbook activities.	Use a deduction to complete workbook activities.	1
	After reading a story, the student puts events from the story in the correct order.	Put events from a textbook story in the correct order.	117
COMPREHENSION SKILLS: REASONING To teach the student to use reasoning skills to understand text	After reading a selection, the student draws conclusions based on evidence from it.	Answer questions about a textbook selection by drawing conclusions.	1
	When presented with a predictive rule, the student uses the rule to predict outcomes.	Complete workbook exercises by using given rules to predict outcomes.	3
	When presented with a classification rule, the student uses it to classify objects.	Complete exercises by using given rules to classify objects.	1
	When presented with the major and minor premises of a formal written deduction, the student completes the deduction by drawing a conclusion.	Write the conclusion for a formal written deduction.	1
	When presented with a passage, the student identifies the author's purpose.	Identify the author's purpose in a passage.	51
	When presented with information previously learned, the student plays a Fact Game to show mastery of the information.	Play the Fact Game.	10–140 every tenth lesson
COMPREHENSION SKILLS: CONTENT KNOWLEDGE To teach students to retain and use content concepts	When presented with content information, the student retains and uses content concepts.	Retain and use content concepts.	1

Teacher Presentation Book Lessons (continued)

LITERARY SKILLS: CHARACTERS AND SETTING To teach the student to understand characters and setting	After reading a story, the student interprets the feelings of a story character.	Answer questions about a textbook story by interpreting a character's feelings.	4
	After reading a story, the student interprets the motives of a story character.	Answer questions about a textbook story by interpreting a character's motives.	4
	After reading a story, the student infers the point of view of a story character.	Answer questions about a textbook story by inferring a character's point of view.	6
	After reading a story, the student plays the role of a story character.	Answer questions about a textbook story by pretending to be a story character.	13
	After reading a story, the student describes the setting of the story.	Describe the setting of a story.	4
LITERARY SKILLS: TYPES OF LITERATURE To teach the student to read a variety of types of literature	When presented with realistic fiction, the student reads it.	Read realistic fiction in the textbook.	41–52,54–63, 68–78
	When presented with fantasy, the student reads it.	Read fantasy in the textbook.	1
	When presented with a non-fiction selection, the student reads it.	Read a non-fiction selection in the textbook.	1
	When presented with an information passage, the student reads it.	Read an information passage in the textbook.	1
	When presented with realism and fantasy, the student distinguishes between them.	Distinguish between realism and fantasy.	1
LITERARY SKILLS: DIALOGUE To teach the student to use punctuation to read and comprehend text	When presented with sentences containing quotation marks, the student identifies what the character said by underlining the correct part.	Underline what a character said.	8
STUDY SKILLS: USING REFERENCE MATERIAL To teach the student to use reference material	When presented with a written question, the student writes the correct answer.	Write answers to questions about a textbook story presented in either the textbook or the workbook.	1
	When presented with an information passage, the student reads it without error.	Read information passages in the textbook.	1
	When presented with a standard measurement (e.g. centimeter, inch) the student identifies the proper use of the measurement.	Complete skill exercises by identifying and applying standard measurements.	8
	When presented with a map, the student interprets it.	Use a given map to answer questions about direction, relative size, proximity, labels, and other map-related concepts from a textbook story.	14
	When presented with a diagram, the student interprets it.	Answer questions about a given diagram.	16
	When presented with a globe, the student interprets it.	Use a globe to answer questions.	46
	When presented with a time line, the student interprets it.	Interpret a time line.	64

	When presented with a blank standard form, the student fills it out correctly.	Complete workbook exercises by filling out standard forms.	79
	When presented with a blank check, the student fills it out correctly.	Complete workbook exercises by filling out a check correctly.	81
	When presented with reference materials, the student uses those materials to write a report.	Use reference materials to write a report.	143
SPECIAL PROJECTS To apply previously learned skills in a new setting	When presented with a Special Project, the student completes it.	Complete the following Special Projects:	After Lesson:
		Make a large map.	23
		Conduct an experiment to show that substances like steel can float on water.	35
		Make a globe of the earth.	52
		Produce a picture based on a text description.	61
		Put on a play about the Trojan War.	67
		Write questions and take notes about a passage; have a guest speaker.	78
		Use research materials to find information about myths.	81
		Make a display about football.	106
		Use reference materials to find information about Australian animals.	122
		Make a word game using synonyms, opposites, and homonyms.	127
		Write a report about Leif Ericson or Eric the Red.	143
		Write a report about George Washington.	144
		Make a time line.	145

Purpose of the track	Behavioral objectives	The student is asked to	First appears in lesson:
WRITING COMPONENT To give the student practice in writing sentences	When presented with a complete sentence, the student copies it correctly.	Copy a sentence correctly.	11
	After reading a story, the student writes a sentence(s) describing the main idea(s).	Write main-idea sentences.	76
SPELLING COMPONENT: WORD SPELLING To give the student practice in spelling sounds and words	When presented with words with regular short vowels, the student spells them correctly.	Write words with regular short vowels.	1
	When presented with words ending with multiple consonants, the student spells them correctly.	Write words ending with multiple consonants.	1
	When presented with words beginning with multiple consonants, the student spells them correctly.	Write words beginning with multiple consonants.	1
	When presented with words with new combinations, the student spells them correctly.	Write words with the following combinations:	
		th	5
		sh	5
		ch	5
		ar	17
		al	17
		ay	19
		or	23
		ol	23
		ea	26
		ck	29
		ou	32
		ll	58
		oi	67
		oy	67
		oo	76
		aw	81
	When presented with words with final E, the student spells them correctly.	Write words with final E.	85

	When presented with compound words, the student spells them correctly.	Write compound words.	135
SPELLING COMPONENT: C-V-C IDENTIFICATION To teach the student to spell words with specific spelling patterns	When presented with words, the student identifies vowels in the words.	Identify vowels in words.	6
	When presented with words, the student identifies Y as a vowel or consonant.	Identify Y as a vowel or consonant.	8
	When presented with words, the student identifies consonants in words as C.	Identify consonants in words as C.	11
	When presented with words, the student identifies C-V-C words.	Identify C-V-C words.	48
SPELLING COMPONENT: ADDING ENDINGS To teach the student to spell words with endings	When presented with regular words, the student adds endings to them.	Add the following endings to regular words:	
		s	37
		ed	44
		ing	44
		er	44
		est	51
		ful	51
		ly	51
		en	102
		less	102
	When presented with C-V-C words, the student adds endings to them.	Add endings to C-V-C words.	101
	When presented with final-E words, the student adds endings to them.	Add the following endings to final-E words:	
		ed	106
		er	107
		ing	114
		en	128

Purpose of the track	Behavioral objectives	The student is asked to	First appears in lesson:
REFERENCE MATERIAL To teach students to use reference material and book parts	When presented with the table of contents, the student reads it and responds to questions based on it.	Read the table of contents and respond to questions based on it	51–60,128–131, 137,139
	When presented with a glossary, the student reads it and responds to questions based on it.	Read the glossary and respond to questions based on it	100–107,126–140
	When presented with guide words, the student reads them and responds to questions based on them.	Read guide words and respond to questions based on them.	100–107,126–140
	When presented with a dictionary, the student uses it to identify the meaning of words.	Use a dictionary to identify the meaning of words.	105–118
	When presented with an index, the student uses it correctly.	Use an index correctly.	119–140
GRAMMAR To teach the student correct grammar	When presented with a subject and a blank, the student writes the correct form of the verb.	Write the correct form of a given verb.	53–57
	When presented with a sentence with a missing word(s), the student writes the correct form of the word(s) in the blank.	Write the correct form of a missing word(s) in the blank.	63–64
ALPHABETICAL ORDER To teach the student to alphabetize words	When presented with a list of words, the student puts them in alphabetical order.	Put words in alphabetical order: First letter Second letter Third letter	 61–66 67–80 81–103
STUDY SKILLS To teach the student use of study skills	When presented with an orally presented passage, the student takes notes on the passage.	Take notes about an orally presented passage.	65
	When presented with categories and a blank outline, the student completes the outline.	Complete an outline about categories.	67-69
	When presented with a topic and an outline, the student completes the outline.	Complete an outline about a topic.	70–72
	When presented with a topic and an outline, the student completes the outline and writes a paragraph.	Complete an outline about a topic and write a paragraph.	73
FACT vs. OPINION To teach the student to identify fact and opinion	When presented with a statement, the student labels the statement as fact or opinion.	Identify statements as fact or opinion.	71

LISTENING SKILLS To teach the student to listen carefully	When presented with rules for good listening, the student reads them.	Read rules for good listening.	72
	After listening to peers read a passage, the student writes questions they would like to ask and critiques the account.	Write questions to ask about a passage and critique the account.	73–88
WRITING To teach the student to write coherent passages	When presented with a topic and an outline, the student completes the outline, writes and edits a paragraph.	Complete an outline about a topic, then write and edit a paragraph.	73
	When presented with a picture, the student writes and edits a story about it.	Write and edit a story about a picture.	75–77,81,83
	When presented with a topic and an outline, the student completes the outline, writes and edits a report.	Complete an outline about a topic, then write and edit a report.	74–81
	When presented with a topic, the student writes and edits a story about it.	Write and edit a story about a given topic.	82–84,86
	When presented with a story, the student uses the story to write a poem.	Write a poem from a story.	85,87,88
TECHNOLOGY To give the student practice in using computers	When presented with a writing assignment, the student uses the computer to complete the assignment.	Use the computer to complete a writing assignment.	81–88
VOCABULARY To teach the student to use a variety of vocabulary	When presented with a word and a prefix, the student learns the meaning of the prefix, and combines the word and prefix to create a new word.	Use the following prefixes: dis re un super	 83 84 87 96
	When presented with a word and a suffix, the student learns the meaning of the suffix, and combines the word and suffix to create a new word.	Use the following suffixes: less ful ness er	89 91 92 94
	When presented with a list of words, the student identifies the root word.	Identify the root word.	104–107
	When presented with an idiomatic expression, the student explains what the expression means.	Explain the meaning of an idiomatic expression.	112–113
	When presented with a simile, the student explains what it means.	Explain the meaning of a simile.	114–115
	When presented with an underlined word, the student uses context to identify the meaning of the word.	Use context to identify the meaning of a given word.	116–118
	When presented with a list of words, the student identifies words that are synonyms.	Match synonyms.	118

Purpose of the track	Behavioral objectives	The student is asked to	First appears in lesson:
ACTIVITIES To apply previously learned skills in a new setting	When presented with an activity, the student completes it.	Complete the following activities: Describe and draw a picture of their favorite pet.	1
		Plan and draw a make-believe animal.	2
		Make up a rule and draw a picture that illustrates the rule.	5
		Measure objects using metric and standard measurement.	11,14
		Make compound words.	13
		Write a story summary.	19
		Draw a map.	26
		Compare sizes of animals and write a short description of one of the animals.	27
		Answer questions about a map.	29
		Compare weights of various items.	33
		Compare frogs and toads.	34
		Read a map and answer questions about distance.	36
		Draw a diagram of a fly and label its parts.	37
		Compare the relative speeds of various animals.	41
		Read a thermometer and answer questions.	43
		Categorize animals as warm-blooded or cold-blooded.	48
		Use a map to compare sizes of various countries.	51
		Draw a poster of an ocean liner sinking at sea, then write a news story about the event.	54

continued	continued		
		Plan for provisions needed for survival on a deserted island.	56
		Draw a diagram of a machine and explain how it works.	59
		Create an advertising poster.	62
		Write interview questions and answers.	63
		Create a time line for their school years.	64
		Use a globe to locate countries.	65
		Draw a model of a Trojan Horse, using math to figure relative sizes.	67
		Identify the senses and make a poster describing each.	68
		Write a paragraph telling about the importance of water as a natural resource.	69
		Practice filling out forms.	79
		Answer questions about the weight and relative strength of four animals.	93
		Write a short newspaper feature about a football player.	98
		Use a map to complete a graphic organizer.	113
		Write a description of a kangaroo.	116
		Create a ship's log for a journey.	117
		Compare minutes and days.	118
		Draw a map of an imaginary country.	119
		Distinguish between pairs of homonyms.	123
		Write contractions and the words they are made from.	127
		Draw the insides of an imaginary time machine.	145

Purpose of the track	Behavioral objectives	The student is asked to	First appears in lesson:
LITERATURE LESSONS To elaborate on skills the student is learning and provide a wide genre of literature	The student reads and participates in activities related to each story in the Literature Lessons.	Read and participate in activities in the following literature selections:	
		Stephanie's Ponytail	10
		George at the Zoo	20
		A House with a Star Inside	30
		Remember	30
		Pop's Truck	40
		Trixie	50
		The Three Wishes	60
		Tom's Friend	70
		The Case of Natty Nat	80
		Swap	80
		The Thirsty Crows	90
		Rabbit	90
		Moonwalker	100
		See the Rabbits—Part 1	110
		See the Rabbits—Part 2	115
		The Proud Crow	120
		The Fox and the Crow	130
		The Magic Teakettle	140

Skills Profile Chart

Student's Name_____ Year _____

Teacher's Name _____

School's Name _____ Phone _____

Student's grade in school:_____

Number of days absent: lessons 1-50 _____   lessons 51-100 _____   lessons 101-145 ___

Last lesson completed _____   Date _____

Comments:

	Lessons 1–70	**Lessons 71–145**
Decoding Activities		
Story Reading		
Comprehension Activities		
Areas of Strength		
Areas of needed improvement		

Recommendations:_____

_____

Conference dates and results:_____

_____

_____

_____

_____

_____

CATEGORIES	SKILLS	FIRST APPEARS IN LESSON	DATE MASTERED
DECODING SKILLS: SOUNDS	Read the following sound combinations correctly:		
	ce	7	
	ou	7	
	ir	7	
	oa	15	
	ar	18	
	al	18	
	aw	18	
	oi	23	
	ee	25	
	ea (long)	25	
	mb	26	
	ew	38	
	ea (short)	115	
DECODING SKILLS: WORDS	Read each word without error.	1	
	Repeat each word, spell each word, then reads each word without error.	1	
	Read words with the following endings:		
	s	1	
	es	1	
	ed	3	
	ing	4	
	y	17	
	tion	18	
	sion	18	
	ly	29	
	er	31	
	n	37	
	th	37	

	's	37	
	est	43	
	ment	53	
	or	69	
	able	75	
	ful	122	
	Read a list of irregularly spelled words.	1	
	Read the underlined part of a word and then read the whole word.	3	
	Read parts of compound words and then read the entire word.	6	
	Orally read a list of words without making an error.	1	
	Read syllables of a word, then read the entire word.	3	
	Read words with the following beginning sound(s):		
	sw	55	
	w	108	
	Write homonym(s) for a given word.	123	
	Identify the correct pronunciation of a homograph.	126	
	Write the two words that make up a given contraction.	127	
DECODING SKILLS: SENTENCES AND STORIES	Read part of a textbook selection aloud.	1	
	Read aloud in pairs.	6	
	Read part of a textbook selection silently.	92	
READING CHECKOUTS	Orally read a specified textbook passage in one minute or less with a minimum of decoding errors.	10–150 every fifth lesson	

Behavioral Objectives

CATEGORIES	SKILLS	FIRST APPEARS IN LESSON	DATE MASTERED
COMPREHENSION SKILLS: READINESS	Follow directions presented orally by the teacher.	1	
	Respond to tasks based on pictures in the textbook.	6	
COMPREHENSION SKILLS: VOCABULARY	Explain the meaning of a defined vocabulary word.	4	
	Use a vocabulary word correctly in a sentence.	4	
	Read proper nouns correctly.	11	
	Read "time" words correctly.	12	
	Choose a word that means the same thing as an underlined word or words.	16	
COMPREHENSION SKILLS: LITERAL COMPREHENSION	Memorize facts and rules presented in the textbook.	1	
	Respond orally to facts and rules.	1	
	Respond in writing to questions in the textbook about facts and rules.	1	
	Complete workbook exercises by recalling facts and rules.	1	
	Answer literal questions about a textbook selection.	1	
	Respond in writing to literal questions in the textbook.	1	
	Complete workbook exercises by answering literal questions.	1	
	Answer questions about a textbook selection by recalling details and events.	1	
	Respond in writing to questions in the textbook about details and events.	1	
	Complete workbook exercises by recalling details and events.	1	
	Answer questions about a textbook selection b identifying literal cause and effect.	1	
	Complete workbook exercises by identifying literal causes and effects.	1	
	Follow written directions.	1	

Comprehensive Activities (continued)

COMPREHENSION SKILLS: INTERPRETIVE COMPREHENSION	Predict the outcome of a textbook story.	1	
	Use a textbook story's title to predict its content.	1	
	Answer questions about a textbook selection by inferring causes and effects.	1	
	Respond in writing to inferential cause and effect questions in the textbook.	1	
	Complete workbook exercises by inferring causes and effects.	1	
	Answer questions about a textbook selection by inferring details and events.	1	
	Respond in writing to inferential detail and event questions in the textbook.	1	
	Complete workbook exercises by inferring details and events.	1	
	Use a deduction to complete workbook activities.	1	
	Put events from a textbook story in the correct order.	117	
COMPREHENSION SKILLS: REASONING	Answer questions about a textbook selection by drawing conclusions.	1	
	Complete workbook exercises by using given rules to predict outcomes.	3	
	Complete exercises by using given rules to classify objects.	1	
	Write the conclusion for a formal written deduction.	1	
	Identify the author's purpose in a passage.	51	
	Play the Fact Game.	10–140 every tenth lesson	
COMPREHENSION SKILLS: CONTENT KNOWLEDGE	Retain and use content concepts	1	

CATEGORIES	SKILLS	FIRST APPEARS IN LESSON	DATE MASTERED
LITERARY SKILLS: CHARACTERS AND SETTING	Answer questions about a textbook story by interpreting a character's feelings.	4	
	Answer questions about a textbook story by interpreting a character's motives.	4	
	Answer questions about a textbook story by inferring a character's point of view.	6	
	Answer questions about a textbook story by pretending to be a story character.	13	
	Describe the setting of a story.	4	
LITERARY SKILLS: TYPES OF LITERATURE	Read realistic fiction in the textbook.	41–52, 54–63, 68–78	
	Read fantasy in the textbook.	1	
	Read a non-fiction selection in the textbook.	1	
	Read an information passage in the textbook.	1	
	Distinguish between realism and fantasy.	1	
QUOTATION MARKS	Underline what a character said.	8	

CATEGORIES	SKILLS	FIRST APPEARS IN LESSON	DATE MASTERED
STUDY SKILLS: USING REFERENCE MATERIAL	White answers to questions about a textbook story presented in either the textbook or the workbook.	1	
	Read information passages in the textbook.	1	
	Complete skill exercises by identifying and applying standard measurements.	8	
	Use a given map to answer questions about direction, relative size, proximity, labels, and other map-related concepts from a textbook story.	14	
	Answer questions about a given diagram.	16	
	Use a globe to answer questions.	46	
	Interpret a timeline.	64	
	Complete workbook exercises by filling out standard forms.	79	
	Complete workbook exercises by filling out a check correctly.	81	
	Use reference materials to write a report.	143	

CATEGORIES	SKILLS	FIRST APPEARS IN LESSON	DATE MASTERED
SPECIAL PROJECTS	Complete the following Special Projects:	After Lesson:	
	Make a large map.	23	
	Conduct an experiment to show that substances like steel can float on water.	35	
	Make a globe of the earth.	52	
	Produce a picture based on a text description.	61	
	Put on a play about the Trojan War.	67	
	Write questions and take notes about a passage; have a guest speaker.	78	
	Use research material to find information about myths.	81	
	Make a display about football.	106	
	Use reference materials to find information about Australian animals.	122	
	Make a word game using synonyms, opposites, and homonyms.	127	
	Write a report about Leif Ericson or Eric the Red.	143	
	Write a report about George Washington.	144	
	Make a time line	145	

CATEGORIES	SKILLS	FIRST APPEARS IN LESSON	DATE MASTERED
WRITING SKILLS	Copy a sentence correctly.	11	
	Write main-idea sentences.	76	
SPELLING SKILLS: WORD SPELLING	Write words with regular short vowels.	1	
	Write words ending with multiple consonants.	1	
	Write words beginning with multiple consonants.	1	
	Write words with the following combinations:		
	th	5	
	sh	5	
	ch	5	
	ar	17	
	al	17	
	ay	19	
	or	23	
	ol	23	
	ea	26	
	ck	29	
	ou	32	
	ll	58	
	oi	67	
	oy	67	
	oo	76	
	aw	81	
	Write words with final E.	85	
	Write compound words.	135	
SPELLING SKILLS: C-V-C IDENTIFICATION	Identify vowels in words.	6	
	Identify Y as a vowel or consonant.	8	
	Identify consonants in words as C.	11	
	Identify C-V-C words.	48	

Writing and Spelling Skills Activities (continued)

SPELLING SKILLS: ADDING ENDINGS	Add the following endings to regular words:		
	s	37	
	ed	44	
	ing	44	
	er	44	
	est	51	
	ful	51	
	ly	51	
	en	102	
	less	102	
	Add endings to C-V-C words.	101	
	Add the following endings to final-E words:		
	ed	106	
	er	107	
	ing	114	
	en	128	

CATEGORIES	SKILLS	FIRST APPEARS IN LESSON	DATE MASTERED
REFERENCE MATERIAL	Read the table of contents and respond to questions based on it	51	
	Read the glossary and respond to questions based on it	100	
	Read guide words and respond to questions based on them.	100	
	Use a dictionary to identify the meaning of words.	105	
	Use an index correctly.	119	
GRAMMAR	Write the correct form of a given verb.	53	
	Write the correct form of a missing word(s) in the blank.	63	
ALPHABETICAL ORDER	Put words in alphabetical order:		
	First letter	61	
	Second letter	67	
	Third letter	81	
STUDY SKILLS	Take notes about an orally presented passage.	65	
	Complete an outline about categories.	67	
	Complete an outline about a topic.	70	
	Complete an outline about a topic and writes a paragraph.	73	
FACT VS. OPINION	Identify statements as fact or opinion.	71	
LISTENING SKILLS	Read rules for good listening.	72	
	Write questions to ask about a passage and critiques the account.	73	
WRITING	Complete an outline about a topic then write and edit a paragraph.	73	
	Write and edit a story about a picture.	75	
	Complete an outline about a topic, then write and edit a report.	74	
	Write and edit a story about a given topic.	82	
	Write a poem from a story.	85	

Language Arts (continued)

TECHNOLOGY	Use the computer to complete a writing assignment.	81	
VOCABULARY	Use the following prefixes:		
	dis	83	
	re	84	
	un	87	
	super	96	
	Use the following suffixes:		
	less	89	
	ful	91	
	ness	92	
	er	94	
	Identify the root word.	104	
	Explain the meaning of an idiomatic expression.	112	
	Explain the meaning of a simile.	114	
	Use context to identify the meaning of a given word.	116	
	Match synonyms.	118	

ACTIVITIES ACROSS THE CURRICULUM

CATEGORIES	SKILLS	FIRST APPEARS IN LESSON	DATE MASTERED
ACTIVITIES ACROSS THE CURRICULUM	Complete an activity in a content area.	51	

CATEGORIES	SKILLS	FIRST APPEARS IN LESSON	DATE MASTERED
LITERATURE LESSONS	Read and participate in activities in the following literature selections:		
	Stephanie's Ponytail	10	
	George at the Zoo	20	
	A House with a Star Inside	30	
	Remember	30	
	Pop's Truck	40	
	Trixie	50	
	The Three Wishes	60	
	Tom's Friend	70	
	The Case of Natty Nat	80	
	Swap	80	
	The Thirsty Crows	90	
	Rabbit	90	
	Moonwalker	100	
	See the Rabbits—Part 1	110	
	See the Rabbits—Part 2	115	
	The Proud Crow	120	
	The Fox and the Crow	130	
	The Magic Teakettle	140	

SRA
Cursive Writing

Grades 2-4 and older students with poor handwriting

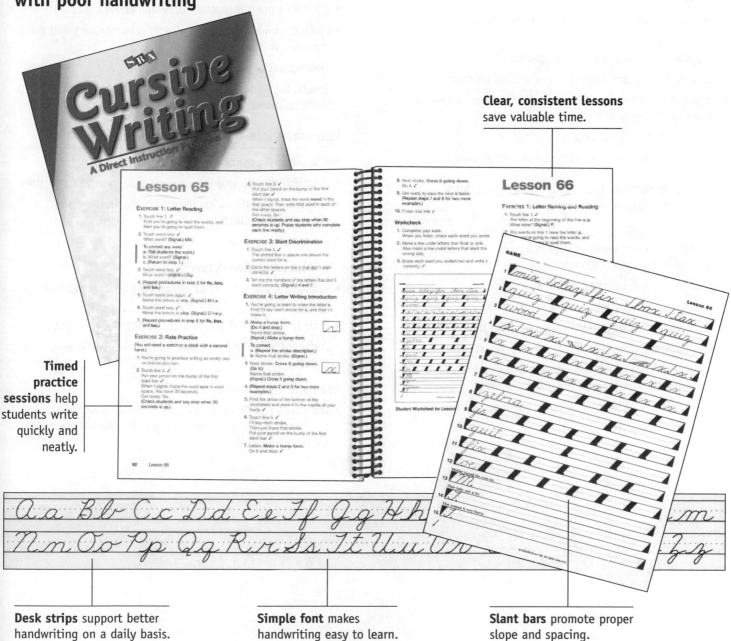

Clear, consistent lessons save valuable time.

Timed practice sessions help students write quickly and neatly.

Desk strips support better handwriting on a daily basis.

Simple font makes handwriting easy to learn.

Slant bars promote proper slope and spacing.

DIRECT SRA INSTRUCTION

The results are proven, the possibilities endless.℠

CURSIVE WRITING
Teach Students to Write with Ease and Confidence

Get the results you want

Whether you work with young students learning cursive for the first time or older students whose handwriting needs improvement, SRA/McGraw-Hill's *Cursive Writing* program makes it easy. In just 20 minutes a day, you can teach your students to:

- Form all uppercase and lowercase letters in isolation, letter groups, and words
- Use proper line placement and spacing
- Identify and correct common handwriting mistakes
- Copy letters, words, sentences, and paragraphs according to specified rate criteria
- Write faster and more legibly
- Read cursive writing and write cursive responses

Tap into practical teaching strategies and program features

The *Cursive Writing* program is finely tuned to help you quickly develop and improve your students' cursive writing. Clear, consistent lesson formats:

- Require minimal preparation time
- Introduce cursive strokes using familiar manuscript letters
- Model letter formation using simple stroke descriptions
- Help students write new letters one stroke at a time
- Increase writing speed through the practice of high-frequency letter combinations and words
- Provide review of learned skills to promote mastery and build independence

Make it easy for students to learn

The *Cursive Writing* program makes handwriting comfortable for students of all ability levels.

- A simplified font reduces frills, making it easy for students to master strokes.
- Slant bars prompt parallel slope and correct spacing.
- Emphasis on high-frequency letter combinations and words increases writing speed.
- Timed practice sessions develop fluency and automaticity.
- Special techniques and planned correction procedures help students overcome poor writing habits.

Use materials that maximize your class time

The **Teacher Presentation Book** contains:

- Detailed, easy-to-use lesson plans that save valuable time
- Practical suggestions and teaching tips for new and experienced instructors
- Reproducible placement tests

The **Student Workbook** provides:

- Valuable support for each lesson that enables students to apply new skills immediately
- Built-in review and practice to promote fluency and mastery
- Gradually faded prompts that make handwriting easy to learn

Additional Components include:

- **Wallcards** and **Desk Strips** that provide convenient visual reinforcement of the handwriting techniques students are learning

Making the Difference™
1-888-SRA-4543
Resources and ordering information at SRAonline.com

SRA

R80001053
1203

The *McGraw·Hill* Companies